Par for the Course- Faith and Fairways

Joshua Rhoades

Published by Joshua Paul Rhoades, 2024.

PAR FOR THE COURSE- FAITH AND FAIRWAYS

First edition. August 26, 2024.

ISBN: 979-8227182364

Written by Joshua Rhoades.

Also by Joshua Rhoades

Courage Under Fire: David's Stand On The Battlefield
Jonah's Journey: Voices Of Redemption And Lessons In Obedience
The Furnace Of Faith: 12 Principles From The Heat Of Faith
Whispers of Hope: Inspiring Stories of Men's Prayers In Scripture
Frontier Legends: The Oregon Dream
Elijah: A Beacon Of Boldness
HOOK, LINE & SAVIOUR - Faith Reflections from Fishing
Driven By Faith: Motor Racing Inspired Christian Life
30 Day Devotional - Bold and Strong- Coffee Devotions for a
Courageous Christian Walk
Authentic Christianity: The Heart of Old Time Religion
Consider The Ant - God's Tiny Preachers
Flee Fornication: The Plea For Purity
Renewed Hope- How to Find Encouragement in God
Sounding The Call - The Voice of Conviction
The Altar - Where Heaven Meets Earth
The Bible's Battlefields- Timeless Lessons from Ancient Wars
The Sacred Art of Silence - How Silence Speaks in Scripture
Under Fire- The Sanctity of the Traditional Biblical Home
Who Is on the Lord's Side? A Call to Righteousness
What Is Truth? - From Skepticism to Submission
First and Goal- Faith and Football Fundamentals
From Dugout to Devotion- Spiritual Lessons from Baseball
Par for the Course- Faith and Fairways
The Believer's Pace- Tools for Running Life's Marathon

The Immutable Fortress- Security in God's Unchanging Nature

Chapter 1 Patience

Chapter 2 Perseverance

Chapter 3 Pressure

Chapter 4 Precision

Chapter 5 Practice

Chapter 6 Patience with Others

Chapter 7 Preparation

Chapter 8 Pace

Chapter 9 Physical Fitness

Chapter 10 Persistence

Chapter 11 Planning

Chapter 12 Pride

Chapter 13 Pressure Situations

Chapter 14 Positivity

Chapter 15 Precision in Putting

Chapter 16 Patience in Adversity

Chapter 17 Peace of Mind

Chapter 18 Proper Technique

Chapter 19 Positive Attitude

Chapter 20 Pressure of Competition

Chapter 21 Partnership

Chapter 22 Precision in Swing

Chapter 23 Perspective

Chapter 24 Prayer

Chapter 25 Perfection

Chapter 1 Patience

Patience is a crucial trait for both golfers and Christians, embodying the ability to wait for the right moment and trusting in the process. For a golfer, patience means waiting for the perfect time to take a shot, carefully considering the conditions and strategy needed for success. On the golf course, there are many moments that require a player to slow down, think through their options, and choose the best approach. Rushing can lead to mistakes, poor shots, and ultimately a higher score. A golfer learns to take their time, aiming for precision and control rather than speed. This might mean waiting for the wind to die down, for the green to clear, or simply taking a few extra moments to calm their nerves and focus on their swing. This patience is practiced over time, as golfers develop their skills and understand that haste often leads to errors. Similarly, in the Christian life, patience is about waiting on God's timing, trusting that He knows what is best for us and that His plans are always perfect. Psalm 27:14 says, "Wait on the LORD: be of good courage, and he shall strengthen thine heart: wait, I say, on the LORD." This verse encourages believers to be courageous in their waiting, knowing that God will provide strength and guidance. Just as a golfer must trust in their training and instincts, Christians must trust in God's wisdom and timing. In life, there are many situations where immediate answers or solutions are not available, and it is during these times that patience becomes essential. Waiting for a job opportunity, for healing, for guidance in difficult decisions, or for the fulfillment of a promise can be challenging, but it is also a time of growth and strengthening of faith.

For a golfer, every game is a test of patience. The sport itself is designed in a way that requires players to remain calm and composed, regardless of how well or poorly they are playing. A single round of golf can take several hours, and within that time, there are numerous opportunities for frustration and impatience to arise. A bad shot, a missed putt, or an unexpected change in weather can all test a player's patience. However, seasoned golfers learn to accept these challenges as part of the game. They understand that each hole offers a new beginning, a chance to improve and make up for previous mistakes. This mindset helps them stay focused and avoid the pitfalls of impatience, such as rushing shots or becoming mentally distracted. Similarly, Christians face various trials and tribulations that test their patience. Life is filled with unexpected challenges and delays that can cause frustration and anxiety. However, the Bible teaches that these trials are opportunities for growth and refinement. James 1:3-4 says, "Knowing this, that the trying of your faith worketh patience. But let patience have her perfect work, that ye may be perfect and entire, wanting nothing." This passage encourages believers to see trials as a means of developing patience, which ultimately leads to spiritual maturity and completeness.

In both golf and the Christian life, patience is also about maintaining a positive attitude and perspective. A golfer who becomes frustrated and impatient is likely to see their performance decline. Negative emotions can cloud judgment, leading to poor decision-making and more mistakes. On the other hand, a patient golfer remains optimistic and focused, even when things are not going well. They recognize that every shot is an opportunity to learn and improve, and they keep their eyes on the ultimate goal. This positive outlook helps them stay calm and composed, which in turn improves their performance. Similarly, Christians are called to maintain a positive attitude, even in the face of difficulties. Romans 12:12 says, "Rejoicing in hope; patient in tribulation; continuing instant in prayer." This verse highlights the importance of hope and prayer in developing patience. By keeping their focus on God's promises and remaining steadfast in prayer, believers can maintain a positive perspective and trust that God is working all things for their good.

Patience in golf also involves careful planning and execution. Before taking a shot, a golfer must consider various factors such as distance, wind speed, terrain, and club selection. This requires a thoughtful and methodical approach, rather than impulsive or rushed decisions. A patient golfer takes the time to assess the situation, make a plan, and execute the shot with precision. This careful planning often leads to better results and fewer mistakes. Similarly, Christians are called to approach their lives with careful planning and reliance on God's guidance. Proverbs 3:5-6 says, "Trust in the LORD with all thine heart; and lean not unto thine own understanding. In all thy ways acknowledge him, and he shall direct thy paths." This passage encourages believers to seek God's wisdom and guidance in all their decisions, trusting that He will lead them in the right direction. By patiently seeking God's will and following His guidance, Christians can make wise decisions and avoid the pitfalls of impulsive actions.

In both golf and the Christian life, patience is also about endurance and perseverance. A golfer must endure the physical and mental demands of the game, remaining focused and determined throughout the entire round. This requires a high level of endurance, as well as the ability to persevere through difficult moments. Similarly, Christians are called to endure and persevere in their faith. Hebrews 12:1 says, "Wherefore seeing we also are compassed about with so great a cloud of witnesses, let us lay aside every weight, and the sin which doth so easily beset us, and let us run with patience the race that is set before us." This verse compares the Christian life to a race, emphasizing the need for endurance and perseverance. By keeping their focus on Christ and relying on His strength, believers can endure the challenges of life and remain steadfast in their faith.

Patience is also about waiting for the right opportunities. In golf, timing is crucial. A golfer must wait for the right moment to take a shot, considering factors such as wind speed, course conditions, and the position of other players. Taking a shot too soon or too late can result in a poor outcome. A patient golfer waits for the optimal moment, ensuring the best possible result. Similarly, Christians are called to wait on God's timing, trusting that He knows the best time for everything. Ecclesiastes 3:1 says, "To every thing there is a season, and a time to every purpose under the heaven." This verse reminds believers that God has a perfect timing for everything in their lives. By waiting on God's timing and trusting His plan, Christians can experience the fullness of His blessings and purposes.

Patience is also about humility and acceptance. In golf, a player must accept that they will not always perform perfectly. Mistakes are inevitable, and a patient golfer learns to accept these mistakes with humility and grace. They do not become discouraged or frustrated, but instead, use their mistakes as opportunities to learn and improve. This humility and acceptance are crucial for long-term success and growth in the game. Similarly, Christians are called to humility and acceptance in their faith journey. James 4:10 says, "Humble yourselves in the sight of the Lord, and he shall lift you up." This verse emphasizes the importance of humility in the Christian life. By accepting their imperfections and relying on God's grace, believers can grow in their faith and experience God's uplifting and strengthening.

Patience also involves trust and confidence. A golfer must trust in their training, skills, and instincts, even when faced with challenging situations. This trust and confidence help them stay calm and focused, improving their chances of success. Similarly, Christians are called to trust in God and have confidence in His promises. Psalm 37:5 says, "Commit thy way unto the LORD; trust also in him; and he shall bring it to pass." This verse encourages believers to trust in God's plan and have confidence that He will fulfill His promises. By placing their trust in God, Christians can experience peace and assurance, even in the face of uncertainties and challenges.

In conclusion, patience is a vital trait for both golfers and Christians, involving the ability to wait for the right moment, maintain a positive attitude, plan carefully, endure challenges, wait for the right opportunities, practice humility and acceptance, and trust in the process. For golfers, patience means waiting for the perfect time to take a shot, carefully considering the conditions and strategy needed for success. For Christians, patience means waiting on God's timing, trusting that He knows what is best and that His plans are always perfect. Psalm 27:14 says, "Wait on the LORD: be of good courage, and he shall strengthen thine heart: wait, I say, on the LORD." This verse encourages believers to be courageous in their waiting, knowing that God will provide strength and guidance. By practicing patience, both golfers and Christians can achieve their goals, grow in their respective journeys, and experience the fullness of their potential.

Chapter 2 Perseverance

Perseverance is a key quality in both golf and the Christian life, representing the ability to continue pressing forward despite challenges and setbacks. For a golfer, perseverance means continuing to play even after a poor start, maintaining focus and determination throughout the entire round. Golf is a sport that requires mental toughness and resilience. A single bad shot or a poor hole can be disheartening, but a true golfer knows that the game is not over until the last putt is made. They must keep their composure, stay focused, and believe in their ability to recover and improve as the game progresses. This ability to persevere is what often separates the good golfers from the great ones. They understand that setbacks are part of the game, and they use these experiences to learn and grow. Similarly, in the Christian life, perseverance means continuing to trust in God and follow His commandments, even when faced with trials and tribulations. James 1:12 states, "Blessed is the man that endureth temptation: for when he is tried, he shall receive the crown of life, which the Lord hath promised to them that love him." This verse highlights the blessings and rewards that come from enduring through difficult times, reminding believers that their perseverance will be rewarded by God.

In both golf and the Christian life, perseverance is not just about enduring difficulties but also about maintaining a positive attitude and a forward-looking perspective. For a golfer, this means staying positive after a bad shot, not letting frustration take over, and focusing on the next opportunity to make a good play. They must remind themselves that every shot is a new chance to improve their score, and every hole is a fresh start. This positive mindset helps golfers to stay motivated and to keep pushing forward, regardless of how the game started. They learn to take each shot one at a time, not dwelling on past mistakes but looking ahead to future opportunities. This same principle applies to the Christian life, where believers are encouraged to stay hopeful and to trust in God's plan, even when facing trials. Romans 5:3-4 says, "And not only so, but we glory in tribulations also: knowing that tribulation worketh patience; and patience, experience; and experience, hope." This passage teaches that trials produce perseverance, and perseverance leads to character and hope. By maintaining a hopeful and positive attitude, Christians can find strength and encouragement to continue their journey of faith.

Perseverance also involves a commitment to continual improvement and growth. In golf, players are always striving to improve their skills, whether it's their swing, putting, or course management. They practice regularly, analyze their performance, and seek feedback from coaches and peers. This dedication to improvement is a form of perseverance, as it requires consistent effort and a willingness to face and overcome challenges. Similarly, Christians are called to grow in their faith and to continually seek to become more like Christ. This requires a commitment to spiritual disciplines such as prayer, Bible study, and fellowship with other believers. Philippians 3:14 captures this pursuit of growth and improvement: "I press toward the mark for the prize of the high calling of God in Christ Jesus." This verse encourages believers to keep striving for spiritual maturity and to never give up, no matter how difficult the journey may be.

Both golfers and Christians must also learn to deal with setbacks and disappointments in a constructive manner. In golf, setbacks can come in the form of a bad round, a missed putt, or an unexpected change in weather conditions. How a golfer responds to these setbacks is crucial. They can either let the setbacks affect their entire game, or they can choose to learn from the experience and move on. Resilience is a key part of perseverance, and resilient golfers are able to bounce back quickly from disappointments. They understand that setbacks are temporary and that perseverance will eventually lead to success. In the Christian life, setbacks can come in many forms, such as personal failures, health issues, or difficult circumstances. Believers are called to trust in God's sovereignty and to remain steadfast in their faith, even when facing setbacks. Romans 8:28 reminds Christians that "all things work together for good to them that love God, to them who are the called according to his purpose." This verse assures believers that God is in control and that He can use even the most difficult situations for their good and His glory.

Perseverance also means staying committed to one's goals and values, regardless of external pressures or challenges. For a golfer, this means staying true to their game plan and not being swayed by the actions of other players or the pressure of competition. They must remain focused on their own performance and trust in their preparation and skills. This commitment to one's goals is essential for long-term success in golf. Similarly, Christians are called to stay committed to their faith and to live according to God's commandments, even when faced with societal pressures or opposition. Galatians 6:9 encourages believers to "not be weary in well doing: for in due season we shall reap, if we faint not." This verse emphasizes the importance of perseverance in doing good and remaining faithful to God's call, promising that the rewards will come in due time.

In both golf and the Christian life, perseverance is closely linked to patience. For a golfer, patience means waiting for the right moment to take a shot, being willing to lay up instead of going for a risky shot, and understanding that improvement takes time. They must be patient with themselves, their progress, and the game itself. This patience is essential for maintaining a steady and focused approach throughout the round. In the Christian life, patience means waiting on God's timing and trusting that His plans are perfect. It involves being patient in prayer, patient in waiting for answers, and patient in enduring hardships. Hebrews 10:36 says, "For ye have need of patience, that, after ye have done the will of God, ye might receive the promise." This verse highlights the necessity of patience in the Christian walk, reminding believers that perseverance and patience go hand in hand.

Perseverance also involves a willingness to make sacrifices and to endure hardships for the sake of a greater goal. In golf, this might mean sacrificing leisure time to practice, enduring physical strain, and pushing through mental fatigue during a long round. Golfers understand that these sacrifices are necessary for improvement and success. Similarly, Christians are called to take up their cross and follow Christ, which often involves making sacrifices and enduring hardships. Luke 9:23 says, "If any man will come after me, let him deny himself, and take up his cross daily, and follow me." This verse calls believers to a life of perseverance, marked by self-denial and a commitment to following Christ, regardless of the cost.

Perseverance is also about faith and trust. A golfer must have faith in their training, their skills, and their ability to succeed. This faith helps them to stay confident and focused, even when faced with challenges. They trust that their hard work will pay off and that they have the ability to overcome obstacles. Similarly, Christians are called to have faith in God and to trust in His promises. Hebrews 11:1 defines faith as "the substance of things hoped for, the evidence of things not seen." This faith is the foundation of perseverance in the Christian life, providing the assurance and confidence needed to endure trials and to continue following God.

Perseverance also involves a community of support. For a golfer, this might include coaches, caddies, family, and friends who provide encouragement, advice, and support. This community helps golfers to stay motivated and to keep pushing forward, even when the going gets tough. Similarly, Christians are part of a community of believers who support and encourage one another. Hebrews 10:24-25 says, "And let us consider one another to provoke unto love and to good works: Not forsaking the assembling of ourselves together, as the manner of some is; but exhorting one another: and so much the more, as ye see the day approaching." This passage highlights the importance of community and mutual encouragement in the Christian life, emphasizing that perseverance is often a collective effort.

In both golf and the Christian life, perseverance is rewarded. For a golfer, the rewards might include personal satisfaction, improved skills, tournament victories, and the respect of peers. These rewards are the result of hard work, dedication, and a never-give-up attitude. Similarly, the Christian life is marked by the promise of eternal rewards for those who persevere. James 1:12 promises, "Blessed is the man that endureth temptation: for when he is tried, he shall receive the crown of life, which the Lord hath promised to them that love him." This verse assures believers that their perseverance will be rewarded by God, not only in this life but also in eternity.

In conclusion, perseverance is a vital quality for both golfers and Christians, involving the ability to continue pressing forward despite challenges and setbacks. For golfers, perseverance means continuing to play even after a poor start, maintaining focus and determination throughout the entire round. For Christians, perseverance means continuing to trust in God and follow His commandments, even when faced with trials and tribulations. James 1:12 states, "Blessed is the man that endureth temptation: for when he is tried, he shall receive the crown of life, which the Lord hath promised to them that love him." This verse highlights the blessings and rewards that come from enduring through difficult times, reminding believers that their perseverance will be rewarded by God. By maintaining a positive attitude, committing to continual improvement, dealing with setbacks constructively, staying committed to their goals, practicing patience, making sacrifices, having faith and trust, relying on community support, and looking forward to the rewards, both golfers and Christians can achieve their goals and fulfill their potential. Perseverance is a journey marked by resilience, dedication, and unwavering commitment, leading to growth, success, and ultimately, the fulfillment of one's purpose.

Chapter 3 Pressure

Pressure is a common experience for both golfers and Christians, and it requires a combination of skill, mental toughness, and faith to handle it effectively. For a golfer, handling the pressure of a critical putt is essential for success. When standing over a putt that could win the tournament, every aspect of the golfer's preparation, focus, and mental strength is put to the test. The weight of expectations, the silence of the crowd, and the importance of the moment can create intense pressure. However, experienced golfers learn to manage this pressure by staying calm, focusing on their routine, and trusting in their skills. They take deep breaths, visualize the ball going into the hole, and block out distractions. This ability to stay composed under pressure often separates the champions from the rest. Similarly, in the Christian life, facing life's pressures with faith is crucial. Life presents various pressures, such as making important decisions, dealing with difficult relationships, or handling financial stress. Christians are called to handle these pressures with faith and reliance on God. Philippians 4:6 says, "Be careful for nothing; but in every thing by prayer and supplication with thanksgiving let your requests be made known unto God." This verse encourages believers to not be anxious but to bring their concerns to God through prayer and thanksgiving, trusting that He will provide guidance and peace.

In both golf and the Christian life, managing pressure involves preparation and practice. For a golfer, this means spending countless hours on the practice green, honing their putting skills, and preparing for high-pressure situations. They simulate tournament conditions, practice with distractions, and develop a routine that helps them stay focused. This preparation builds confidence and muscle memory, enabling them to perform under pressure. Similarly, Christians prepare for life's pressures by developing a strong spiritual foundation through regular prayer, Bible study, and worship. These practices help believers build a deep relationship with God, understand His promises, and develop trust in His guidance. Just as a golfer practices putting to be ready for a critical moment, Christians cultivate their faith to be ready for life's challenges.

Another key aspect of handling pressure is maintaining focus. For a golfer, this means blocking out distractions, such as the crowd, the leaderboard, or negative thoughts. They focus on the task at hand, taking it one shot at a time. This intense focus helps them stay in the moment and execute their shots with precision. Similarly, Christians are called to maintain focus on God and His promises, especially during stressful times. Hebrews 12:2 encourages believers to "look unto Jesus the author and finisher of our faith; who for the joy that was set before him endured the cross, despising the shame, and is set down at the right hand of the throne of God." By focusing on Jesus and His example, Christians can find strength and encouragement to handle pressure.

In both golf and the Christian life, managing pressure also involves having a positive mindset. For a golfer, a positive mindset means believing in their ability to make the putt, even if they have missed similar shots in the past. They visualize success, speak positively to themselves, and stay optimistic. This positive mindset helps them stay calm and confident. Similarly, Christians are called to maintain a positive mindset by trusting in God's goodness and faithfulness. Romans 8:28 says, "And we know that all things work together for good to them that love God, to them who are the called according to his purpose." This verse reminds believers that God is working for their good, even in difficult situations, and encourages them to stay hopeful and positive.

Another important aspect of handling pressure is having a support system. For a golfer, this support system includes their caddie, coach, family, and friends. These individuals provide encouragement, advice, and emotional support, helping the golfer stay grounded and focused.

Similarly, Christians rely on their faith community for support during stressful times. Fellow believers, pastors, and spiritual mentors offer prayer, encouragement, and practical support, helping Christians navigate life's pressures. Hebrews 10:24-25 emphasizes the importance of community: "And let us consider one another to provoke unto love and to good works: Not forsaking the assembling of ourselves together, as the manner of some is; but exhorting one another: and so much the more, as ye see the day approaching." This passage highlights the importance of mutual support and encouragement in handling life's pressures.

In both golf and the Christian life, handling pressure also involves trusting in a higher power. For a golfer, this might mean trusting in their training and preparation, as well as the guidance of their coach. They believe that their hard work and practice will pay off, and they trust their instincts and skills. Similarly, Christians are called to trust in God and His plan for their lives. Proverbs 3:5-6 says, "Trust in the LORD with all thine heart; and lean not unto thine own understanding. In all thy ways acknowledge him, and he shall direct thy paths." This verse encourages believers to trust in God's wisdom and guidance, especially when facing pressure and uncertainty.

Both golfers and Christians also learn to handle pressure by accepting that mistakes and setbacks are part of the journey. In golf, even the best players miss putts and make errors. What sets them apart is their ability to recover and move forward. They don't dwell on mistakes but learn from them and focus on the next shot. This resilience is crucial for handling pressure effectively. Similarly, Christians understand that life is full of challenges and setbacks, but they are called to persevere and trust in God's grace. 2 Corinthians 12:9 says, "And he said unto me, My grace is sufficient for thee: for my strength is made perfect in weakness." This verse reminds believers that God's grace is sufficient to help them through their weaknesses and challenges.

In both golf and the Christian life, handling pressure also involves staying calm and composed. For a golfer, staying calm under pressure means taking deep breaths, following a pre-shot routine, and keeping a steady mind. This composure helps them make clear decisions and execute their shots effectively. Similarly, Christians are encouraged to remain calm and trust in God's peace during stressful times. Philippians 4:7 says, "And the peace of God, which passeth all understanding, shall keep your hearts and minds through Christ Jesus." This verse assures believers that God's peace will guard their hearts and minds, helping them stay calm and composed under pressure.

Handling pressure in both golf and the Christian life also involves setting realistic expectations. For a golfer, this means understanding that not every putt will go in, and not every round will be perfect. They set achievable goals and focus on continuous improvement rather than perfection. Similarly, Christians are called to set realistic expectations for their spiritual journey, understanding that growth takes time and that they will face challenges along the way. Philippians 3:13-14 encourages believers to press on towards their goals: "Brethren, I count not myself to have apprehended: but this one thing I do, forgetting those things which are behind, and reaching forth unto those things which are before, I press toward the mark for the prize of the high calling of God in Christ Jesus." This passage encourages believers to keep striving for spiritual maturity, even when faced with pressure and setbacks.

In both golf and the Christian life, handling pressure involves using the right tools and resources. For a golfer, this means having the right equipment, such as a reliable putter, and using techniques and strategies that have been practiced and refined. Similarly, Christians are equipped with spiritual tools and resources, such as the Bible, prayer, and the guidance of the Holy Spirit, to help them handle life's pressures. Ephesians 6:11-18 describes the full armor of God, which includes truth, righteousness, the gospel of peace, faith, salvation, and the Word of God. By using these spiritual tools, believers can stand firm and handle pressure effectively.

Handling pressure also involves learning from past experiences. For a golfer, each round and each putt provides valuable lessons that can be applied in future situations. They review their performance, identify areas for improvement, and adjust their strategies accordingly. Similarly, Christians learn from their past experiences and apply these lessons to their spiritual journey. Romans 5:3-4 says, "And not only so, but we glory in tribulations also: knowing that tribulation worketh patience; and patience, experience; and experience, hope." This passage highlights the importance of learning from tribulations and gaining experience that builds hope and perseverance.

In both golf and the Christian life, handling pressure also involves maintaining a sense of perspective. For a golfer, this means remembering that golf is just a game and that there are more important things in life. This perspective helps them stay grounded and not become overwhelmed by the pressure. Similarly, Christians are encouraged to maintain an eternal perspective, focusing on God's kingdom and the bigger picture. Colossians 3:2 says, "Set your affection on things above, not on things on the earth." This verse reminds believers to keep their focus on heavenly things, which helps them handle earthly pressures with a sense of peace and purpose.

Finally, handling pressure in both golf and the Christian life involves celebrating successes and learning from failures. For a golfer, making a critical putt under pressure is a cause for celebration, and missing a putt is an opportunity to learn and improve. Similarly, Christians are called to rejoice in their successes and to see failures as opportunities for growth. Philippians 4:4 encourages believers to "Rejoice in the Lord always: and again I say, Rejoice." This verse highlights the importance of maintaining a joyful and thankful heart, regardless of the pressures and challenges faced.

In conclusion, handling pressure is a crucial skill for both golfers and Christians, involving preparation, focus, a positive mindset, support systems, trust, resilience, calmness, realistic expectations, the right tools and resources, learning from experiences, maintaining perspective, and celebrating successes. For a golfer, handling the pressure of a critical putt is essential for success, requiring mental toughness and composure. Similarly,

Christians are called to handle life's pressures with faith, relying on God's guidance and peace. Philippians 4:6 says, "Be careful for nothing; but in every thing by prayer and supplication with thanksgiving let your requests be made known unto God." This verse encourages believers to not be anxious but to bring their concerns to God through prayer and thanksgiving, trusting that He will provide guidance and peace. By developing these skills and relying on their faith, both golfers and Christians can handle pressure effectively and achieve their goals.

Chapter 4 Precision

Precision is a crucial element in both golf and the Christian life, representing the accuracy and careful attention needed to achieve success and live righteously. For a golfer, hitting the ball with precision is essential for a good game. Each shot must be carefully calculated, considering factors such as wind speed, distance, terrain, and the type of club used. A golfer must focus intently on their form, grip, stance, and swing to ensure the ball goes exactly where they intend. This level of precision requires consistent practice, discipline, and a deep understanding of the game. Golfers spend countless hours on the driving range and putting green, honing their skills and striving for greater accuracy. They analyze their performance, seek feedback from coaches, and make adjustments to improve their precision. This meticulous approach helps them achieve lower scores and perform well in competitions. Similarly, in the Christian life, living according to God's word requires precision. Christians are called to study the Bible diligently, understand its teachings, and apply them accurately in their daily lives. 2 Timothy 2:15 says, "Study to shew thyself approved unto God, a workman that needeth not to be ashamed, rightly dividing the word of truth." This verse emphasizes the importance of studying God's word carefully and living it out with precision, ensuring that one's actions align with God's will.

In both golf and the Christian life, precision involves a commitment to continuous learning and improvement. For a golfer, this means regularly practicing their swing, analyzing their shots, and learning from their mistakes. They seek to understand the mechanics of their swing, the nuances of different courses, and the best strategies for different situations. This commitment to learning helps them refine their skills and achieve greater accuracy. Similarly, Christians are called to continually grow in their knowledge of God's word and deepen their relationship with Him. This involves regular Bible study, prayer, and seeking wisdom from spiritual mentors and teachers. By committing to this process of learning and growth, Christians can better understand God's will and live according to His teachings with greater precision.

Precision in golf also requires focus and concentration. A golfer must block out distractions, stay mentally sharp, and focus on the task at hand. Whether it's a drive from the tee, an approach shot to the green, or a delicate putt, each shot demands the golfer's full attention and concentration. This ability to focus helps them execute their shots with accuracy and avoid costly mistakes. Similarly, Christians are called to stay focused on God and His word, avoiding distractions that can lead them away from His path. Hebrews 12:2 encourages believers to "look unto Jesus the author and finisher of our faith." By keeping their focus on Jesus and His example, Christians can live with precision and avoid the distractions and temptations that can lead them astray.

Precision in both golf and the Christian life also involves careful planning and intentionality. For a golfer, this means planning each shot carefully, considering the conditions and choosing the best strategy. They must think ahead, anticipate challenges, and make intentional decisions to achieve their goals. This careful planning helps them navigate the course effectively and avoid unnecessary risks. Similarly, Christians are called to live intentionally, making decisions that align with God's will and purpose for their lives. Proverbs 3:5-6 says, "Trust in the LORD with all thine heart; and lean not unto thine own understanding. In all thy ways acknowledge him, and he shall direct thy paths." This passage encourages believers to seek God's guidance in all their decisions, ensuring that their actions are intentional and aligned with His will.

Another important aspect of precision is discipline. For a golfer, discipline means consistently practicing, maintaining a proper routine, and staying committed to improving their game. This discipline helps them develop the skills and accuracy needed to perform well. Similarly, Christians are called to practice spiritual disciplines such as prayer,

Bible study, worship, and fellowship. These disciplines help believers grow in their faith, understand God's word more deeply, and live according to His teachings. 1 Timothy 4:7-8 says, "But refuse profane and old wives' fables, and exercise thyself rather unto godliness. For bodily exercise profiteth little: but godliness is profitable unto all things, having promise of the life that now is, and of that which is to come." This passage highlights the importance of spiritual discipline and its role in living a precise and godly life.

Precision also involves accountability. For a golfer, this means being honest about their performance, seeking feedback from coaches, and being accountable for their mistakes. This accountability helps them identify areas for improvement and make necessary adjustments. Similarly, Christians are called to be accountable to one another, seeking guidance and support from fellow believers and being honest about their struggles and shortcomings. James 5:16 says, "Confess your faults one to another, and pray one for another, that ye may be healed. The effectual fervent prayer of a righteous man availeth much." This verse emphasizes the importance of accountability and mutual support in the Christian life, helping believers live with precision and integrity.

In both golf and the Christian life, precision also requires resilience. A golfer will inevitably face challenges and setbacks, such as missed shots, difficult lies, or bad weather conditions. Resilience helps them stay focused, learn from their mistakes, and keep striving for accuracy. Similarly, Christians face trials and challenges in their spiritual journey, but resilience helps them stay committed to God's word and continue living according to His teachings. James 1:2-4 says, "My brethren, count it all joy when ye fall into divers temptations; knowing this, that the trying of your faith worketh patience. But let patience have her perfect work, that ye may be perfect and entire, wanting nothing." This passage encourages believers to remain resilient and steadfast in their faith, trusting that perseverance will lead to spiritual maturity and precision in living out God's word.

Precision in both golf and the Christian life also involves humility. A golfer must be humble enough to acknowledge their mistakes, accept feedback, and be willing to make changes. This humility helps them stay open to learning and improvement. Similarly, Christians are called to live with humility, recognizing their dependence on God and being open to His guidance and correction. Micah 6:8 says, "He hath shewed thee, O man, what is good; and what doth the LORD require of thee, but to do justly, and to love mercy, and to walk humbly with thy God?" This verse highlights the importance of humility in the Christian life, helping believers live with precision and alignment with God's will.

Another key aspect of precision is perseverance. For a golfer, perseverance means continuing to practice and strive for accuracy, even when progress is slow or setbacks occur. They understand that achieving precision takes time and consistent effort. Similarly, Christians are called to persevere in their faith, continually seeking to live according to God's word, even when faced with difficulties. Galatians 6:9 says, "And let us not be weary in well doing: for in due season we shall reap, if we faint not." This verse encourages believers to keep persevering, trusting that their efforts to live a precise and godly life will be rewarded.

Precision in both golf and the Christian life also involves consistency. A golfer must be consistent in their practice, approach, and execution to achieve precision. They develop routines and habits that help them perform accurately under various conditions. Similarly, Christians are called to be consistent in their faith, maintaining regular spiritual practices and living out God's word in all areas of their lives. 1 Corinthians 15:58 says, "Therefore, my beloved brethren, be ye stedfast, unmoveable, always abounding in the work of the Lord, forasmuch as ye know that your labour is not in vain in the Lord." This passage encourages believers to be consistent and steadfast in their faith, knowing that their efforts are valuable and meaningful.

In both golf and the Christian life, precision also involves clarity of purpose. A golfer must have a clear understanding of their goals and what they need to do to achieve them. This clarity helps them stay focused and motivated. Similarly, Christians are called to have a clear sense of their purpose and calling in life, understanding God's will and striving to fulfill it. Ephesians 2:10 says, "For we are his workmanship, created in Christ Jesus unto good works, which God hath before ordained that we should walk in them." This verse highlights the importance of understanding and living out God's purpose for our lives with precision.

Precision also involves adaptability. A golfer must be able to adapt to changing conditions on the course, such as weather, terrain, and the performance of their opponents. This adaptability helps them maintain accuracy and perform well under various circumstances. Similarly, Christians are called to be adaptable in their faith, responding to life's changes and challenges with wisdom and faithfulness. Philippians 4:12-13 says, "I know both how to be abased, and I know how to abound: every where and in all things I am instructed both to be full and to be hungry, both to abound and to suffer need. I can do all things through Christ which strengtheneth me." This passage emphasizes the importance of adaptability and reliance on Christ's strength in living a precise and godly life.

In conclusion, precision is a vital quality for both golfers and Christians, involving accuracy, focus, discipline, resilience, humility, perseverance, consistency, clarity of purpose, and adaptability. For a golfer, hitting the ball with precision is essential for a good game, requiring careful calculation, consistent practice, and a deep understanding of the sport. Similarly, in the Christian life, living according to God's word requires precision, involving diligent study, application of biblical principles, and reliance on God's guidance. 2 Timothy 2:15 says, "Study to shew thyself approved unto God, a workman that needeth not to be ashamed, rightly dividing the word of truth." By committing to precision in their respective pursuits, both golfers and Christians can achieve their goals, grow in their skills and faith, and fulfill their potential. Precision is a journey marked by continuous learning, focus, discipline, and a commitment to excellence, leading to success and fulfillment in both golf and the Christian life.

Chapter 5 Practice

Practice is a fundamental aspect of both golf and the Christian life, representing the regular, dedicated efforts needed to improve skills and grow spiritually. For a golfer, regular practice is essential to improving their skills. This involves spending countless hours on the driving range, putting green, and course, honing their swing, refining their putting technique, and mastering various aspects of the game. A golfer practices their grip, stance, swing mechanics, and mental focus, all with the goal of achieving greater accuracy, consistency, and confidence. They understand that improvement comes through repetition and that every practice session is an opportunity to learn and grow. They also seek feedback from coaches, watch instructional videos, and analyze their performance to identify areas for improvement. This dedication to regular practice is what allows golfers to develop their skills, lower their scores, and perform well in competitions. Similarly, in the Christian life, regular spiritual practice is essential for growth and maturity. Christians are called to engage in regular practices such as prayer, Bible study, worship, and fellowship to deepen their relationship with God and strengthen their faith. 1 Timothy 4:7 says, "But refuse profane and old wives' fables, and exercise thyself rather unto godliness." This verse emphasizes the importance of spiritual discipline and regular practice in developing godliness and living a life that pleases God.

In both golf and the Christian life, practice is about more than just repetition; it involves intentionality and a focus on improvement. For a golfer, this means practicing with specific goals in mind, such as improving their short game, increasing their driving distance, or lowering their putting average. They approach each practice session with a plan, focusing on particular aspects of their game and working systematically to improve. This intentionality helps them make the most of their practice time and achieve measurable progress. Similarly, Christians are called to engage in spiritual practices with intentionality, focusing on specific areas of their spiritual life and seeking to grow in their relationship with God. This might involve setting aside regular times for prayer and Bible study, participating in worship and fellowship, and seeking opportunities to serve others. By approaching spiritual practices with intentionality, Christians can grow in their faith and develop a deeper understanding of God's will for their lives.

Practice also involves perseverance and dedication. For a golfer, this means continuing to practice even when progress is slow or setbacks occur. They understand that improvement takes time and that consistent effort is required to achieve their goals. This dedication helps them stay motivated and committed to their practice routine, even when it is challenging. Similarly, Christians are called to persevere in their spiritual practices, even when they face difficulties or feel discouraged. Galatians 6:9 encourages believers to "not be weary in well doing: for in due season we shall reap, if we faint not." This verse reminds Christians that their efforts to grow spiritually will be rewarded and that perseverance is essential for spiritual growth.

In both golf and the Christian life, practice also involves learning from others. For a golfer, this might mean seeking guidance from a coach, taking lessons, or learning from more experienced players. They understand that others can provide valuable insights and feedback that can help them improve their game. Similarly, Christians are called to learn from spiritual mentors, teachers, and fellow believers. Ephesians 4:11-13 says, "And he gave some, apostles; and some, prophets; and some, evangelists; and some, pastors and teachers; for the perfecting of the saints, for the work of the ministry, for the edifying of the body of Christ: till we all come in the unity of the faith, and of the knowledge of the Son of God, unto a perfect man, unto the measure of the stature of the fulness of Christ." This passage highlights the importance of learning from others within the Christian community and the role of spiritual leaders in helping believers grow in their faith.

Practice also involves patience and grace. For a golfer, this means being patient with themselves as they work to improve their skills, understanding that progress takes time and that setbacks are a natural part of the learning process. They also learn to extend grace to themselves, not becoming discouraged by mistakes but using them as opportunities to learn and grow. Similarly, Christians are called to be patient with themselves as they seek to grow spiritually. They understand that spiritual growth is a lifelong journey and that they will face challenges and setbacks along the way. They also learn to extend grace to themselves, trusting in God's forgiveness and relying on His strength to help them continue growing. Philippians 1:6 says, "Being confident of this very thing, that he which hath begun a good work in you will perform it until the day of Jesus Christ." This verse reminds believers that God is at work in their lives and that He will continue to help them grow and mature in their faith.

In both golf and the Christian life, practice also involves consistency. For a golfer, this means maintaining a regular practice schedule and committing to practice even when it is inconvenient or challenging. Consistency helps them develop good habits and build the muscle memory needed for accurate and confident performance. Similarly, Christians are called to be consistent in their spiritual practices, maintaining regular times for prayer, Bible study, worship, and fellowship. Consistency helps believers develop a deep and abiding relationship with God and strengthens their faith. 1 Corinthians 15:58 says, "Therefore, my beloved brethren, be ye stedfast, unmoveable, always abounding in the work of the Lord, forasmuch as ye know that your labour is not in vain in the Lord." This passage encourages believers to be steadfast and consistent in their spiritual practices, knowing that their efforts are valuable and meaningful.

In both golf and the Christian life, practice also involves humility. For a golfer, this means being humble enough to recognize their weaknesses and areas for improvement, and being open to feedback and guidance from others. This humility helps them stay teachable and willing to learn, which is essential for growth. Similarly, Christians are called to live with humility, recognizing their need for God's guidance and being open to His correction and instruction. James 4:10 says, "Humble yourselves in the sight of the Lord, and he shall lift you up." This verse highlights the importance of humility in the Christian life and the promise that God will lift up those who humble themselves before Him.

Practice also involves accountability. For a golfer, this might mean being accountable to a coach, practice partner, or mentor who can provide encouragement, feedback, and support. Accountability helps them stay motivated and committed to their practice routine. Similarly, Christians are called to be accountable to one another, seeking support and encouragement from fellow believers. Hebrews 10:24-25 says, "And let us consider one another to provoke unto love and to good works: not forsaking the assembling of ourselves together, as the manner of some is; but exhorting one another: and so much the more, as ye see the day approaching." This passage emphasizes the importance of mutual support and accountability within the Christian community, helping believers stay committed to their spiritual practices and grow in their faith.

In both golf and the Christian life, practice also involves setting goals and measuring progress. For a golfer, this means setting specific, achievable goals for their practice sessions and tracking their progress over time. This helps them stay focused and motivated, and provides a sense of accomplishment as they see their improvement. Similarly, Christians are called to set spiritual goals and measure their progress in their faith journey. This might involve setting goals for regular Bible reading, prayer, or service, and reflecting on their growth and progress over time. Philippians 3:13-14 says, "Brethren, I count not myself to have apprehended: but this one thing I do, forgetting those things which are behind, and reaching forth unto those things which are before, I press toward the mark for the prize of the high calling of God in Christ Jesus." This passage encourages believers to set goals and strive for spiritual growth, always pressing forward in their faith journey.

In conclusion, practice is a vital aspect of both golf and the Christian life, involving regular, dedicated efforts to improve skills and grow spiritually. For a golfer, regular practice involves honing their swing, refining their putting technique, and mastering various aspects of the game. This requires intentionality, perseverance, learning from others, patience, grace, consistency, humility, accountability, and goal-setting. Similarly, in the Christian life, regular spiritual practice involves engaging in prayer, Bible study, worship, and fellowship to deepen one's relationship with God and strengthen one's faith. 1 Timothy 4:7 says, "But refuse profane and old wives' fables, and exercise thyself rather unto godliness." By committing to regular practice in their respective pursuits, both golfers and Christians can achieve their goals, grow in their skills and faith, and fulfill their potential. Practice is a journey marked by continuous learning, dedication, and a commitment to growth, leading to success and fulfillment in both golf and the Christian life.

Chapter 6 Patience with Others

Patience with others is an important trait for both golfers and Christians, embodying the ability to tolerate and support those around us despite differences and challenges. For a golfer, being patient with slower players is essential. Golf is a game that can vary greatly in pace, and often players will find themselves waiting for others to take their shots. This waiting can test a golfer's patience, especially if they are eager to continue playing or are focused on maintaining their rhythm. However, experienced golfers understand the importance of being patient and respectful toward other players. They recognize that everyone plays at their own pace and that the course should be a supportive environment for all. This patience is not just about waiting quietly but also about maintaining a positive attitude and showing encouragement. It involves using the waiting time productively, such as visualizing the next shot, discussing strategy with a caddie, or simply enjoying the surroundings. This approach helps to maintain harmony on the course and ensures that all players have an enjoyable experience. Similarly, in the Christian life, being patient with others is a core value. Christians are called to show patience and love toward others, even when it is difficult. Ephesians 4:2 says, "With all lowliness and meekness, with longsuffering, forbearing one another in love." This verse encourages believers to be humble, gentle, and patient, bearing with one another in love. This patience is crucial in building and maintaining healthy relationships within the community and reflecting God's love to others.

In both golf and the Christian life, patience with others involves understanding and empathy. For a golfer, this means recognizing that every player has their own challenges and strengths. Some may be new to the game, others may be working through a slump, and some may have different playing styles that affect their pace. By understanding these differences, a golfer can show empathy and support, rather than frustration or impatience. They can offer encouragement, share tips, and help create a positive atmosphere on the course. Similarly, Christians are called to understand and empathize with others. Life is full of diverse experiences and backgrounds, and each person's journey is unique. By understanding the struggles and perspectives of others, Christians can offer genuine support and love. Romans 12:15 says, "Rejoice with them that do rejoice, and weep with them that weep." This verse highlights the importance of sharing in the experiences of others, showing empathy, and building strong, compassionate relationships.

Patience with others also requires self-control. For a golfer, this means controlling any frustration or impatience that may arise when waiting for slower players. It involves maintaining composure and not letting negative emotions affect their game. This self-control is essential for staying focused and performing well. Similarly, Christians are called to exercise self-control in their interactions with others. This means refraining from anger, criticism, or harsh words, even when faced with challenging behavior. Proverbs 15:1 says, "A soft answer turneth away wrath: but grievous words stir up anger." This verse emphasizes the power of gentle and kind words in diffusing tension and fostering patience and understanding.

Another aspect of patience with others is grace and forgiveness. For a golfer, this might mean forgiving a fellow player for a mistake that slowed down the game or disrupted their concentration. It involves letting go of any resentment and moving forward with a positive attitude. Similarly, Christians are called to show grace and forgiveness to others. Ephesians 4:32 says, "And be ye kind one to another, tenderhearted, forgiving one another, even as God for Christ's sake hath forgiven you." This verse highlights the importance of forgiving others, just as God has forgiven us, and showing kindness and compassion in all interactions.

Patience with others also involves encouragement and support. For a golfer, this means offering words of encouragement to slower players, helping them feel more confident and relaxed. It involves creating a supportive environment where everyone feels valued and respected. Similarly, Christians are called to encourage and support one another. 1 Thessalonians 5:11 says, "Wherefore comfort yourselves together, and edify one another, even as also ye do." This verse encourages believers to build each other up and provide comfort and support, fostering a strong and loving community.

In both golf and the Christian life, patience with others is also about leading by example. For a golfer, this means demonstrating patience and respect on the course, setting a positive example for others to follow. By modeling good behavior, they can influence others to do the same, creating a more harmonious and enjoyable environment for all players. Similarly, Christians are called to be examples of patience and love. 1 Peter 2:21 says, "For even hereunto were ye called: because Christ also suffered for us, leaving us an example, that ye should follow his steps." This verse reminds believers to follow the example of Christ, who demonstrated ultimate patience and love, even in the face of suffering.

Patience with others also involves active listening and communication. For a golfer, this means listening to the concerns or questions of fellow players and communicating effectively to ensure everyone is on the same page. Good communication helps to prevent misunderstandings and fosters a cooperative spirit on the course. Similarly, Christians are called to be good listeners and communicators. James 1:19 says, "Wherefore, my beloved brethren, let every man be swift to hear, slow to speak, slow to wrath." This verse emphasizes the importance of listening carefully, speaking thoughtfully, and controlling anger, all of which are key to practicing patience with others.

In both golf and the Christian life, patience with others also involves humility. For a golfer, this means recognizing that everyone has room for improvement and that no one is perfect. It involves being humble enough to offer help without condescension and to accept that others may have different approaches or needs. Similarly, Christians are called to live with humility, recognizing their own imperfections and being willing to serve and support others. Philippians 2:3 says, "Let nothing be done through strife or vainglory; but in lowliness of mind let each esteem other better than themselves." This verse encourages believers to act with humility and to value others above themselves, fostering a spirit of patience and mutual respect.

Patience with others also requires perseverance. For a golfer, this means continuing to show patience and support throughout the entire round, even if it becomes challenging. It involves staying committed to a positive and respectful attitude, regardless of the circumstances. Similarly, Christians are called to persevere in their patience with others. Galatians 6:9 says, "And let us not be weary in well doing: for in due season we shall reap, if we faint not." This verse encourages believers to keep doing good, including showing patience and kindness, trusting that their efforts will bear fruit in time.

In both golf and the Christian life, patience with others also involves recognizing and celebrating progress. For a golfer, this means acknowledging and celebrating the improvements and successes of fellow players, no matter how small. It involves encouraging others to keep striving and improving. Similarly, Christians are called to recognize and celebrate the growth and achievements of others. Romans 12:10 says, "Be kindly affectioned one to another with brotherly love; in honour preferring one another." This verse encourages believers to honor and celebrate each other, fostering a supportive and patient community.

In conclusion, patience with others is a vital quality for both golfers and Christians, involving understanding, empathy, self-control, grace, forgiveness, encouragement, support, leading by example, active listening, communication, humility, perseverance, and celebrating progress. For a golfer, being patient with slower players is essential for maintaining harmony on the course and ensuring an enjoyable experience for all. This involves understanding and empathizing with the challenges of others, exercising self-control, showing grace and forgiveness, offering encouragement and support, setting a positive example, listening and communicating effectively, practicing humility, persevering in patience, and celebrating progress. Similarly, in the Christian life, being patient with others is crucial for building and maintaining healthy relationships and reflecting God's love. Ephesians 4:2 says, "With all lowliness and meekness, with longsuffering, forbearing one another in love." By committing to these principles, both golfers and Christians can foster positive and supportive environments, build strong relationships, and live in a way that honors God and reflects His love to others. Patience with others is a journey marked by continuous growth, dedication, and a commitment to love and support those around us, leading to fulfilling and harmonious experiences in both golf and the Christian life.

Chapter 7 Preparation

Preparation is a key component in both golf and the Christian life, representing the efforts and steps taken to ensure success and readiness for upcoming challenges. For a golfer, preparing for each round involves meticulous planning and practice. Before stepping onto the course, a golfer will typically spend hours on the driving range and putting green, working on their swing, refining their short game, and ensuring that their equipment is in top condition. They may study the course layout, considering the placement of hazards, the slope of the greens, and the best strategies for each hole. This preparation helps them to feel confident and ready to face the various challenges that the course may present. Golfers understand that proper preparation can make the difference between a successful round and a disappointing one. They know that by putting in the effort beforehand, they can reduce the likelihood of mistakes and improve their chances of performing well. Similarly, in the Christian life, preparation is essential for facing spiritual battles and living a life that honors God. Christians are called to prepare for the challenges and temptations they will encounter by putting on the full armor of God. Ephesians 6:11 says, "Put on the whole armour of God, that ye may be able to stand against the wiles of the devil." This verse emphasizes the importance of being spiritually prepared, equipping oneself with God's truth, righteousness, peace, faith, salvation, and the word of God to stand firm against spiritual attacks.

In both golf and the Christian life, preparation involves a commitment to continuous learning and improvement. For a golfer, this means regularly practicing their skills, analyzing their performance, and seeking ways to improve. They may take lessons from a coach, study instructional videos, and engage in exercises to enhance their strength and flexibility. This dedication to learning helps them to develop a deeper understanding of the game and to refine their techniques. Similarly, Christians are called to continually grow in their knowledge of God's word and to seek spiritual growth. This involves regular Bible study, prayer, and participation in church activities. By committing to these practices, believers can deepen their relationship with God and better understand His will for their lives.

Preparation in both golf and the Christian life also involves mental readiness. For a golfer, this means developing a strong mental game, which is crucial for handling the pressures and challenges of a round. They work on their focus, concentration, and mental resilience, using techniques such as visualization and positive self-talk to stay calm and confident. This mental preparation helps them to remain composed under pressure and to make thoughtful decisions on the course. Similarly, Christians are called to prepare their minds for spiritual battles by renewing their minds with God's truth. Romans 12:2 says, "And be not conformed to this world: but be ye transformed by the renewing of your mind, that ye may prove what is that good, and acceptable, and perfect, will of God." This verse emphasizes the importance of mental and spiritual preparation, encouraging believers to align their thoughts with God's word and to be transformed by His truth.

In both golf and the Christian life, preparation also involves equipping oneself with the right tools and resources. For a golfer, this means ensuring that they have the appropriate clubs, balls, and other equipment. They may also use technology such as rangefinders and swing analyzers to enhance their preparation. Having the right tools can significantly impact their performance and help them to navigate the course more effectively. Similarly, Christians are called to equip themselves with spiritual tools to face life's challenges. This includes putting on the full armor of God, as mentioned in Ephesians 6:11, which consists of the belt of truth, the breastplate of righteousness, the shoes of the gospel of peace, the shield of faith, the helmet of salvation, and the sword of the Spirit, which is the word of God. These spiritual tools help believers to stand firm against the enemy and to live victoriously.

Preparation in both golf and the Christian life also involves planning and strategy. For a golfer, this means developing a game plan for each round, considering the course layout, weather conditions, and their own strengths and weaknesses. They may decide on specific strategies for each hole, such as aiming for certain targets or choosing particular clubs for different shots. This strategic planning helps them to navigate the course more effectively and to minimize risks. Similarly, Christians are called to plan and be strategic in their spiritual lives. This might involve setting spiritual goals, developing a plan for regular prayer and Bible study, and seeking accountability and support from fellow believers. Proverbs 21:5 says, "The thoughts of the diligent tend only to plenteousness; but of every one that is hasty only to want." This verse highlights the importance of diligent planning and preparation, encouraging believers to be thoughtful and intentional in their spiritual lives.

In both golf and the Christian life, preparation also involves being adaptable and flexible. For a golfer, this means being prepared to adjust their strategy and approach based on changing conditions, such as unexpected weather changes or unforeseen challenges on the course. They must be able to think on their feet and make quick decisions to adapt to new situations. Similarly, Christians are called to be adaptable and flexible in their spiritual lives, being open to God's leading and willing to adjust their plans as He directs. Proverbs 16:9 says, "A man's heart deviseth his way: but the LORD directeth his steps." This verse reminds believers that while it is important to plan and prepare, they must also be willing to follow God's guidance and be flexible in their approach.

Preparation in both golf and the Christian life also involves perseverance and dedication. For a golfer, this means committing to regular practice and preparation, even when it is challenging or inconvenient. They understand that consistent effort and perseverance are necessary to achieve their goals. Similarly, Christians are called to persevere in their spiritual practices, remaining faithful and dedicated even when faced with difficulties or discouragement. Galatians 6:9 says, "And let us not be weary in well doing: for in due season we shall reap, if we faint not." This verse encourages believers to keep persevering in their preparation and spiritual practices, trusting that their efforts will bear fruit in due time.

In both golf and the Christian life, preparation also involves humility and a willingness to learn from others. For a golfer, this means being humble enough to recognize their weaknesses and to seek guidance and feedback from coaches and more experienced players. This humility helps them to stay open to learning and improvement. Similarly, Christians are called to live with humility, recognizing their need for God's guidance and being willing to learn from spiritual mentors and fellow believers. James 1:21 says, "Wherefore lay apart all filthiness and superfluity of naughtiness, and receive with meekness the engrafted word, which is able to save your souls." This verse emphasizes the importance of humility and a teachable spirit in the Christian life.

Preparation in both golf and the Christian life also involves setting goals and measuring progress. For a golfer, this means setting specific, achievable goals for their practice and performance and tracking their progress over time. This helps them to stay focused and motivated, and provides a sense of accomplishment as they see their improvement. Similarly, Christians are called to set spiritual goals and measure their progress in their faith journey. This might involve setting goals for regular Bible reading, prayer, or service, and reflecting on their growth and progress over time. Philippians 3:13-14 says, "Brethren, I count not myself to have apprehended: but this one thing I do, forgetting those things which are behind, and reaching forth unto those things which are before, I press toward the mark for the prize of the high calling of God in Christ Jesus." This passage encourages believers to set goals and strive for spiritual growth, always pressing forward in their faith journey.

In conclusion, preparation is a vital aspect of both golf and the Christian life, involving regular, dedicated efforts to ensure readiness and success. For a golfer, preparing for each round involves meticulous planning, practice, mental readiness, equipping oneself with the right tools, strategic planning, adaptability, perseverance, humility, setting goals, and measuring progress. Similarly, in the Christian life, preparation involves regular spiritual practices, mental and spiritual readiness, equipping oneself with God's armor, strategic planning, adaptability, perseverance, humility, setting goals, and measuring progress. Ephesians 6:11 says, "Put on the whole armour of God, that ye may be able to stand against the wiles of the devil." By committing to preparation in their respective pursuits, both golfers and Christians can achieve their goals, grow in their skills and faith, and fulfill their potential. Preparation is a journey marked by continuous learning, dedication, and a commitment to growth, leading to success and fulfillment in both golf and the Christian life.

Chapter 8 Pace

Pace is an essential aspect in both golf and the Christian life, signifying the importance of maintaining a steady, consistent effort to achieve long-term success and fulfillment. For a golfer, maintaining a steady pace throughout a round is crucial for achieving good scores and enjoying the game. Golf is a sport that requires a balance of patience, focus, and rhythm. If a golfer rushes their shots or gets frustrated with delays, it can lead to mistakes and poor performance. On the other hand, if they take too long, it can disrupt their flow and concentration. Therefore, finding the right pace is key. This involves developing a consistent pre-shot routine, staying calm and composed between shots, and managing time effectively. Golfers often use the time between shots to plan their next move, visualize successful outcomes, and stay mentally engaged. This steady pace helps them to stay focused, reduce stress, and perform at their best.

Similarly, in the Christian life, running the race of faith with endurance requires maintaining a steady spiritual pace. The Bible compares the Christian life to a race, emphasizing the need for perseverance and steady progress. Hebrews 12:1 says, "Let us run with patience the race that is set before us." This verse encourages believers to approach their faith journey with patience and endurance, recognizing that it is a long-term commitment that requires consistent effort. Just as a runner needs to pace themselves to finish a marathon, Christians need to develop a sustainable spiritual rhythm. This involves regular practices such as prayer, Bible study, worship, and fellowship, which help believers stay connected to God and grow in their faith over time. Maintaining a steady spiritual pace means avoiding the extremes of spiritual burnout or complacency. It's about finding a balanced approach that allows for continuous growth and resilience in the face of challenges. In both golf and the Christian life, maintaining a steady pace also involves managing emotions and staying mentally composed.

For a golfer, this means keeping calm under pressure, not getting discouraged by bad shots, and avoiding the temptation to rush or panic. Emotional control is vital for maintaining a steady pace and making thoughtful decisions on the course. Similarly, Christians are called to manage their emotions and stay composed, especially when facing trials and tribulations. Philippians 4:6-7 says, "Be careful for nothing; but in every thing by prayer and supplication with thanksgiving let your requests be made known unto God. And the peace of God, which passeth all understanding, shall keep your hearts and minds through Christ Jesus." This passage encourages believers to turn to God in prayer, trust in His peace, and maintain emotional stability, which is essential for running the race of faith with endurance.

Another important aspect of maintaining a steady pace is setting realistic goals and expectations. For a golfer, this means understanding their current skill level and setting achievable targets for improvement. Unrealistic expectations can lead to frustration and disappointment, while realistic goals provide motivation and a sense of accomplishment. Golfers often break down their goals into manageable steps, such as improving their putting accuracy or increasing their driving distance, and they celebrate small victories along the way. Similarly, Christians are called to set realistic spiritual goals and expectations. This might involve setting goals for regular Bible reading, prayer, or community service, and recognizing that spiritual growth is a gradual process. Galatians 6:9 says, "And let us not be weary in well doing: for in due season we shall reap, if we faint not." This verse encourages believers to keep pursuing their spiritual goals with perseverance, trusting that their efforts will bear fruit in due time.

Maintaining a steady pace also involves understanding and respecting one's limits. For a golfer, this means knowing when to push hard and when to conserve energy. Overexerting oneself can lead to fatigue and mistakes, while pacing oneself properly ensures consistent performance throughout the round. Golfers learn to listen to their bodies, take breaks when needed, and manage their energy levels effectively. Similarly, Christians are called to recognize their limitations and to rely on God's strength. Isaiah 40:31 says, "But they that wait upon the LORD shall renew their strength; they shall mount up with wings as eagles; they shall run, and not be weary; and they shall walk, and not faint." This verse reminds believers that their strength comes from God and that by trusting in Him, they can maintain the endurance needed for their spiritual journey.

In both golf and the Christian life, maintaining a steady pace also involves resilience and the ability to recover from setbacks. For a golfer, this means bouncing back from a bad shot or a tough hole without letting it affect the rest of their game. Resilience helps golfers stay focused on the present and keep their overall performance on track. They learn to view mistakes as opportunities for learning and growth rather than failures. Similarly, Christians are called to be resilient in their faith, trusting that God can use even difficult circumstances for their good. Romans 8:28 says, "And we know that all things work together for good to them that love God, to them who are the called according to his purpose." This verse encourages believers to trust in God's sovereignty and to remain steadfast in their faith, even when facing challenges.

Maintaining a steady pace also involves consistency in practice and preparation. For a golfer, this means adhering to a regular practice schedule, working on different aspects of their game, and staying disciplined in their training. Consistency in practice helps golfers develop muscle memory, refine their techniques, and build confidence. Similarly, Christians are called to be consistent in their spiritual practices, such as prayer, Bible study, and worship. Consistency helps believers stay connected to God, grow in their faith, and be prepared for spiritual challenges. 1 Corinthians 15:58 says, "Therefore, my beloved brethren, be ye stedfast, unmoveable, always abounding in the work of the Lord, forasmuch as ye know that your labour is not in vain in the Lord." This verse encourages believers to be steadfast and consistent in their spiritual efforts, knowing that their work for the Lord is valuable and meaningful.

In both golf and the Christian life, maintaining a steady pace also involves being patient and trusting the process. For a golfer, this means understanding that improvement takes time and that progress may be gradual. They stay committed to their practice and trust that their efforts will eventually pay off. This patience helps them stay motivated and avoid frustration. Similarly, Christians are called to be patient in their spiritual growth, trusting that God is at work in their lives even when progress seems slow. James 1:4 says, "But let patience have her perfect work, that ye may be perfect and entire, wanting nothing." This verse encourages believers to allow patience to work in their lives, leading to spiritual maturity and completeness.

Maintaining a steady pace also involves having a supportive community. For a golfer, this might include coaches, mentors, and fellow players who provide encouragement, feedback, and support. A strong support system helps golfers stay motivated and navigate challenges. Similarly, Christians are called to be part of a supportive faith community. Fellow believers, church leaders, and spiritual mentors provide encouragement, accountability, and support, helping Christians maintain their spiritual pace and grow in their faith. Hebrews 10:24-25 says, "And let us consider one another to provoke unto love and to good works: Not forsaking the assembling of ourselves together, as the manner of some is; but exhorting one another: and so much the more, as ye see the day approaching." This passage emphasizes the importance of community and mutual encouragement in the Christian life.

In both golf and the Christian life, maintaining a steady pace also involves self-discipline. For a golfer, this means adhering to a practice schedule, making healthy lifestyle choices, and staying focused on their goals. Self-discipline helps golfers stay committed to their training and perform consistently on the course. Similarly, Christians are called to practice self-discipline in their spiritual lives, making choices that align with God's will and staying focused on their spiritual goals. 2 Timothy 1:7 says, "For God hath not given us the spirit of fear; but of power, and of love, and of a sound mind." This verse emphasizes the importance of self-discipline and a sound mind in the Christian life, helping believers maintain their spiritual pace and live according to God's purpose.

In conclusion, maintaining a steady pace is a vital aspect of both golf and the Christian life, involving consistent effort, emotional and mental composure, realistic goals and expectations, understanding and respecting limits, resilience, consistency in practice, patience, supportive community, and self-discipline. For a golfer, maintaining a steady pace throughout a round is crucial for achieving good scores and enjoying the game. This involves developing a consistent pre-shot routine, staying calm and composed, managing time effectively, and balancing patience, focus, and rhythm. Similarly, in the Christian life, running the race of faith with endurance requires maintaining a steady spiritual pace. Hebrews 12:1 says, "Let us run with patience the race that is set before us." By committing to these principles, both golfers and Christians can achieve their goals, grow in their skills and faith, and fulfill their potential. Maintaining a steady pace is a journey marked by continuous learning, dedication, and a commitment to growth, leading to success and fulfillment in both golf and the Christian life.

Chapter 9 Physical Fitness

Physical fitness is a crucial aspect in both golf and the Christian life, highlighting the importance of maintaining and caring for the body to achieve optimal performance and well-being. For a golfer, staying physically fit is essential to play better and improve their game. Golf may seem like a leisurely sport, but it requires a significant amount of physical strength, flexibility, and endurance. Golfers need to have a strong core to maintain balance and stability during their swing, powerful leg muscles to generate force, and flexible joints to ensure a full range of motion. Regular physical exercise, including strength training, cardiovascular workouts, and flexibility exercises, helps golfers enhance their physical capabilities and reduce the risk of injuries. Golfers often follow a fitness regimen that includes exercises specifically designed to improve their swing mechanics and overall fitness. This might involve activities such as weight lifting, running, yoga, and stretching. By staying physically fit, golfers can increase their swing speed, improve their accuracy, and maintain their stamina throughout a round, leading to better performance and lower scores.

Similarly, in the Christian life, taking care of the body as a temple is emphasized in the Bible. Christians are called to honor God with their bodies, recognizing that they are temples of the Holy Spirit. 1 Corinthians 6:19-20 says, "What? know ye not that your body is the temple of the Holy Ghost which is in you, which ye have of God, and ye are not your own? For ye are bought with a price: therefore glorify God in your body, and in your spirit, which are God's." This verse underscores the importance of treating the body with respect and care, as it is a vessel for the Holy Spirit. Taking care of the body involves making healthy lifestyle choices, such as eating nutritious foods, exercising regularly, getting enough sleep, and avoiding harmful behaviors. By maintaining physical fitness, Christians can enhance their overall well-being, increase their energy levels, and be better equipped to serve God and others.

In both golf and the Christian life, physical fitness is also linked to mental and emotional well-being. For a golfer, staying physically fit helps to improve concentration, reduce stress, and boost confidence. Physical exercise releases endorphins, which are chemicals in the brain that act as natural mood lifters. This can help golfers stay positive and focused during a round, even when faced with challenging shots or tough conditions. Mental clarity and emotional stability are crucial for making strategic decisions and maintaining composure on the course. Similarly, Christians are encouraged to care for their physical health as it contributes to their mental and emotional well-being. When the body is healthy and strong, it positively impacts the mind and spirit. Physical fitness can help reduce anxiety, improve mood, and enhance cognitive function, all of which are important for a balanced and fulfilling life. By taking care of their bodies, Christians can better manage stress, stay focused on their spiritual goals, and maintain a positive outlook on life.

Another important aspect of physical fitness is the discipline and self-control it requires. For a golfer, maintaining physical fitness involves a commitment to regular exercise, a balanced diet, and a healthy lifestyle. It requires discipline to stick to a fitness routine, make healthy food choices, and avoid habits that can negatively impact performance. This discipline translates to better focus and perseverance on the golf course. Similarly, Christians are called to practice self-control and discipline in caring for their bodies. Galatians 5:22-23 lists self-control as one of the fruits of the Spirit, emphasizing its importance in the Christian life. By exercising self-control in their physical health, Christians can develop a disciplined lifestyle that honors God and promotes overall well-being.

Physical fitness also involves understanding the body's needs and limitations. For a golfer, this means recognizing when to push harder and when to rest. Overtraining can lead to injuries and burnout, so it's important for golfers to listen to their bodies and allow time for recovery. This balance between training and rest helps to optimize performance and prevent long-term damage. Similarly, Christians are encouraged to understand and respect their bodies' needs and limitations. This involves getting adequate rest, seeking medical care when needed, and practicing self-care. Psalm 127:2 says, "It is vain for you to rise up early, to sit up late, to eat the bread of sorrows: for so he giveth his beloved sleep." This verse highlights the importance of rest and trusting in God's provision. By taking care of their physical health, Christians can ensure that they have the strength and energy to fulfill God's purposes for their lives.

In both golf and the Christian life, physical fitness is also about setting goals and striving for improvement. For a golfer, this might mean setting specific fitness goals, such as increasing flexibility, building strength, or improving endurance. These goals provide motivation and direction, helping golfers to stay committed to their fitness regimen. Tracking progress and celebrating achievements along the way can also boost motivation and confidence. Similarly, Christians are encouraged to set goals for their physical health and work towards them with dedication. This might involve setting goals for regular exercise, healthy eating, or weight management. Philippians 3:14 says, "I press toward the mark for the prize of the high calling of God in Christ Jesus." This verse encourages believers to strive for their goals with perseverance, recognizing that physical fitness is an important aspect of honoring God and living a balanced life.

Physical fitness in both golf and the Christian life also involves community and support. For a golfer, having a support system can make a significant difference in maintaining a fitness routine. This might include working with a fitness trainer, joining a golf fitness group, or having workout partners who provide encouragement and accountability. A supportive community can help golfers stay motivated and committed to their fitness goals. Similarly, Christians are called to support and encourage one another in their physical health journeys. Hebrews 10:24-25 says, "And let us consider one another to provoke unto love and to good works: not forsaking the assembling of ourselves together, as the manner of some is; but exhorting one another: and so much the more, as ye see the day approaching." This passage emphasizes the importance of community and mutual encouragement. By supporting one another in their efforts to maintain physical fitness, Christians can create a positive and motivating environment that promotes overall well-being.

In both golf and the Christian life, physical fitness is also a way of glorifying God. For a golfer, staying physically fit allows them to play their best and enjoy the game to the fullest. It demonstrates a commitment to excellence and a respect for the physical abilities God has given them. Similarly, Christians are called to glorify God in their bodies by taking care of their physical health. 1 Corinthians 10:31 says, "Whether therefore ye eat, or drink, or whatsoever ye do, do all to the glory of God." This verse reminds believers that every aspect of their lives, including their physical health, should be dedicated to glorifying God. By maintaining physical fitness, Christians can honor God, serve others more effectively, and live out their faith in a holistic and balanced way.

In conclusion, physical fitness is a vital aspect of both golf and the Christian life, involving maintaining and caring for the body to achieve optimal performance and well-being. For a golfer, staying physically fit is essential for playing better, enhancing strength, flexibility, and endurance, and reducing the risk of injuries. This involves regular exercise, a balanced diet, and a commitment to a healthy lifestyle. Similarly, in the Christian life, taking care of the body as a temple involves making healthy choices, exercising regularly, and practicing self-control and discipline. 1 Corinthians 6:19-20 says, "What? know ye not that your body is the temple of the Holy Ghost which is in you, which ye have of God, and ye are not your own? For ye are bought with a price: therefore glorify God in your body, and in your spirit, which are God's." By committing to physical fitness, both golfers and Christians can enhance their overall well-being, increase their energy levels, and be better equipped to achieve their goals and fulfill their potential. Physical fitness is a journey marked by continuous effort, dedication, and a commitment to growth, leading to success and fulfillment in both golf and the Christian life.

Chapter 10 Persistence

Persistence is a vital quality for both golfers and Christians, representing the determination to keep going and improving despite setbacks and challenges. For a golfer, persistence means continuing to work on their game even when progress is slow or when they face difficulties. Golf is a challenging sport that requires a lot of practice and dedication. A golfer may spend countless hours on the driving range, refining their swing, working on their putting, and learning how to navigate different courses. There will inevitably be days when their performance is not up to par, when they miss crucial shots, or when they face tough conditions that test their skills and patience. However, a persistent golfer does not give up in the face of these challenges. They analyze their performance, learn from their mistakes, and make adjustments to improve. They understand that setbacks are a natural part of the learning process and that persistence is key to long-term improvement. This mindset helps them stay motivated and committed to their goals, knowing that with continued effort, they can overcome obstacles and achieve success. Similarly, in the Christian life, persistence in faith is crucial, especially when facing challenges and difficulties. Christians are called to remain steadfast in their faith, even when they encounter trials and temptations. Galatians 6:9 says, "And let us not be weary in well doing: for in due season we shall reap, if we faint not." This verse encourages believers to keep doing good and to persist in their faith, trusting that their efforts will be rewarded in God's perfect timing.

In both golf and the Christian life, persistence involves maintaining a positive attitude and staying focused on the end goal. For a golfer, this means keeping a positive mindset even after a bad round or a missed shot. They remind themselves of their long-term goals and stay focused on the process of improvement rather than getting discouraged by temporary setbacks. This positive attitude helps them to stay motivated and to continue working hard. Similarly, Christians are called to maintain a positive attitude and to stay focused on their faith, even when facing difficulties. Philippians 4:13 says, "I can do all things through Christ which strengtheneth me." This verse reminds believers that they can overcome challenges through Christ's strength and that persistence in faith will lead to spiritual growth and maturity.

Persistence also involves resilience and the ability to bounce back from setbacks. For a golfer, resilience means not letting a bad hole or a poor shot affect the rest of their game. They learn to quickly recover from mistakes, refocus, and continue playing to the best of their ability. This resilience is developed through practice and experience, as golfers learn to handle pressure and stay calm under stress. Similarly, Christians are called to be resilient in their faith, trusting that God is with them in every situation and that He will help them overcome challenges. James 1:2-4 says, "My brethren, count it all joy when ye fall into divers temptations; knowing this, that the trying of your faith worketh patience. But let patience have her perfect work, that ye may be perfect and entire, wanting nothing." This passage encourages believers to see trials as opportunities for growth and to develop resilience through perseverance.

In both golf and the Christian life, persistence also involves a willingness to learn and grow. For a golfer, this means continually seeking to improve their skills, learning from coaches and mentors, and staying open to new techniques and strategies. Golfers who are persistent in their pursuit of excellence are always looking for ways to enhance their performance and to overcome weaknesses. This dedication to learning and growth helps them to steadily improve and to achieve their goals. Similarly, Christians are called to continually seek spiritual growth and to learn from God's word and from the wisdom of other believers. 2 Peter 3:18 says, "But grow in grace, and in the knowledge of our Lord and Saviour Jesus Christ. To him be glory both now and for ever. Amen." This verse emphasizes the importance of growth in the Christian life and encourages believers to persist in their pursuit of a deeper relationship with God.

Persistence also involves setting goals and working towards them with determination. For a golfer, setting specific, achievable goals helps to provide direction and motivation. Whether it's improving their putting accuracy, lowering their handicap, or winning a tournament, having clear goals helps golfers to stay focused and to measure their progress. They break down their goals into manageable steps and celebrate their achievements along the way. Similarly, Christians are called to set spiritual goals and to work towards them with determination. This might involve setting goals for regular Bible reading, prayer, or serving in their community. Philippians 3:14 says, "I press toward the mark for the prize of the high calling of God in Christ Jesus." This verse encourages believers to persist in their pursuit of spiritual goals, knowing that their efforts will be rewarded by God.

In both golf and the Christian life, persistence also involves seeking support and encouragement from others. For a golfer, having a support system can make a significant difference in their ability to stay persistent. This might include working with a coach, practicing with a group, or receiving encouragement from friends and family. A supportive community can provide valuable feedback, motivation, and accountability, helping golfers to stay committed to their goals. Similarly, Christians are called to support and encourage one another in their faith. Hebrews 10:24-25 says, "And let us consider one another to provoke unto love and to good works: not forsaking the assembling of ourselves together, as the manner of some is; but exhorting one another: and so much the more, as ye see the day approaching." This passage emphasizes the importance of community and mutual encouragement in the Christian life. By supporting one another, believers can help each other to stay persistent in their faith and to grow spiritually.

Persistence in both golf and the Christian life also involves trust and reliance on a higher power. For a golfer, this means trusting in their training, their skills, and the process of improvement. It involves having faith that their hard work will pay off and that they have the ability to achieve their goals. Similarly, Christians are called to trust in God and to rely on His strength and guidance. Proverbs 3:5-6 says, "Trust in the LORD with all thine heart; and lean not unto thine own understanding. In all thy ways acknowledge him, and he shall direct thy paths." This verse encourages believers to place their trust in God and to rely on His wisdom and direction. By trusting in God, Christians can find the strength and courage to persist in their faith, even when faced with challenges.

In both golf and the Christian life, persistence also involves celebrating progress and acknowledging achievements. For a golfer, celebrating small victories and recognizing improvement helps to maintain motivation and to stay committed to their goals. This might involve celebrating a personal best score, a successful shot, or reaching a fitness milestone. Similarly, Christians are called to celebrate their spiritual growth and to give thanks for God's blessings. Psalm 126:3 says, "The LORD hath done great things for us; whereof we are glad." This verse reminds believers to acknowledge and celebrate the good things that God has done in their lives. By celebrating progress, Christians can stay motivated and encouraged in their faith journey.

In conclusion, persistence is a vital quality for both golfers and Christians, involving the determination to keep going and improving despite setbacks and challenges. For a golfer, persistence means continuing to work on their game, maintaining a positive attitude, being resilient, willing to learn and grow, setting goals, seeking support, trusting in their training, and celebrating progress. Similarly, in the Christian life, persistence in faith involves remaining steadfast, maintaining a positive attitude, developing resilience, seeking spiritual growth, setting goals, seeking support, trusting in God, and celebrating progress. Galatians 6:9 says, "And let us not be weary in well doing: for in due season we shall reap, if we faint not." By committing to persistence in their respective pursuits, both golfers and Christians can achieve their goals, grow in their skills and faith, and fulfill their potential. Persistence is a journey marked by continuous effort, dedication, and a commitment to growth, leading to success and fulfillment in both golf and the Christian life.

Chapter 11 Planning

Planning is a critical aspect of both golf and the Christian life, emphasizing the importance of strategizing and making thoughtful decisions to achieve success and fulfill one's purpose. For a golfer, strategizing each shot is essential to playing well and navigating the course effectively. Golf is a game of precision and careful planning, where every shot requires consideration of various factors, including the distance to the hole, the wind direction, the lie of the ball, and the position of hazards such as bunkers and water. A skilled golfer will take the time to analyze these factors and devise a strategy for each shot, aiming to place the ball in the best possible position for the next stroke. This process involves choosing the right club, determining the optimal swing, and visualizing the desired outcome. Planning each shot helps golfers minimize risks, avoid mistakes, and make the most of their opportunities on the course. Similarly, in the Christian life, making plans aligned with God's will is crucial for living a life that honors Him and fulfills His purposes. Christians are encouraged to seek God's guidance in all their plans and decisions, recognizing that He knows what is best for their lives. Proverbs 16:9 says, "A man's heart deviseth his way: but the LORD directeth his steps." This verse highlights the importance of submitting one's plans to God and trusting Him to direct their steps.

In both golf and the Christian life, planning involves setting goals and creating a roadmap to achieve them. For a golfer, setting specific goals, such as improving their putting accuracy or lowering their handicap, provides direction and motivation. These goals help golfers stay focused and committed to their practice and training routines. They may create a detailed plan that outlines the steps they need to take to reach their goals, including specific drills, practice schedules, and performance benchmarks. Similarly, Christians are called to set spiritual goals and develop plans to achieve them. This might involve setting goals for regular Bible reading, prayer, serving in the community, or personal growth in specific areas of their faith. By creating a plan that outlines the steps needed to achieve these goals, believers can stay focused and motivated in their spiritual journey.

Planning in both golf and the Christian life also involves flexibility and adaptability. For a golfer, this means being prepared to adjust their strategy based on changing conditions, such as unexpected weather changes or challenging course layouts. Flexibility allows golfers to adapt their plans and make necessary adjustments to stay on course. Similarly, Christians are called to be flexible and adaptable in their plans, recognizing that God's plans may differ from their own. Proverbs 19:21 says, "There are many devices in a man's heart; nevertheless the counsel of the LORD, that shall stand." This verse reminds believers that while they may have many plans, it is ultimately God's purpose that prevails. Being open to God's guidance and willing to adjust one's plans according to His will is essential for living a life that honors Him.

Another important aspect of planning is foresight and anticipation. For a golfer, this means thinking ahead and considering the potential outcomes of each shot. They anticipate possible challenges and plan their strategy accordingly to avoid hazards and position themselves advantageously for future shots. This foresight helps golfers make informed decisions and avoid unnecessary risks. Similarly, Christians are called to exercise foresight in their planning, considering the long-term impact of their decisions and actions. Luke 14:28 says, "For which of you, intending to build a tower, sitteth not down first, and counteth the cost, whether he have sufficient to finish it?" This verse emphasizes the importance of planning and considering the cost before embarking on a project or making a significant decision. By exercising foresight and anticipating potential challenges, believers can make wise and informed decisions that align with God's will.

In both golf and the Christian life, planning also involves seeking guidance and wisdom from others. For a golfer, this might mean consulting with a coach or mentor who can provide valuable insights and feedback on their game. Coaches can help golfers develop effective strategies, refine their techniques, and improve their overall performance. Similarly, Christians are called to seek guidance and wisdom from spiritual mentors, pastors, and fellow believers. Proverbs 15:22 says, "Without counsel purposes are disappointed: but in the multitude of counsellors they are established." This verse highlights the importance of seeking wise counsel and the value of receiving input from others. By seeking guidance from trusted individuals, believers can gain valuable perspectives and make more informed decisions in their planning.

Planning in both golf and the Christian life also involves discipline and commitment. For a golfer, this means sticking to their practice schedule, following through with their training plan, and staying focused on their goals. Discipline helps golfers stay committed to their preparation and consistently work towards improving their game. Similarly, Christians are called to practice discipline in their spiritual lives, staying committed to their spiritual practices and following through with their plans. 1 Corinthians 9:24-25 says, "Know ye not that they which run in a race run all, but one receiveth the prize? So run, that ye may obtain. And every man that striveth for the mastery is temperate in all things. Now they do it to obtain a corruptible crown; but we an incorruptible." This passage encourages believers to run their race with discipline and perseverance, striving for the eternal reward.

Another important aspect of planning is setting priorities. For a golfer, this means prioritizing their practice time, focusing on areas of their game that need improvement, and balancing their training with other commitments. Setting priorities helps golfers allocate their time and resources effectively, ensuring that they make progress towards their goals. Similarly, Christians are called to set priorities in their spiritual lives, focusing on what is most important and aligning their actions with God's will. Matthew 6:33 says, "But seek ye first the kingdom of God, and his righteousness; and all these things shall be added unto you." This verse emphasizes the importance of prioritizing God's kingdom and righteousness above all else. By setting priorities and aligning their actions with God's will, believers can ensure that their plans and efforts are focused on what truly matters.

Planning in both golf and the Christian life also involves perseverance and resilience. For a golfer, this means staying committed to their plan, even when faced with setbacks or challenges. They understand that improvement takes time and that persistence is key to achieving their goals. Perseverance helps golfers stay motivated and continue working towards their objectives, even when progress is slow. Similarly, Christians are called to persevere in their faith and stay committed to their spiritual plans, even when faced with difficulties. James 1:12 says, "Blessed is the man that endureth temptation: for when he is tried, he shall receive the crown of life, which the Lord hath promised to them that love him." This verse encourages believers to persevere through trials and remain steadfast in their faith, trusting that their efforts will be rewarded.

In both golf and the Christian life, planning also involves reflection and evaluation. For a golfer, this means regularly assessing their performance, reviewing their progress, and making adjustments to their strategy as needed. Reflection helps golfers identify areas for improvement and refine their plans to achieve better results. Similarly, Christians are called to reflect on their spiritual journey, evaluate their progress, and make necessary adjustments to their plans. Psalm 139:23-24 says, "Search me, O God, and know my heart: try me, and know my thoughts: And see if there be any wicked way in me, and lead me in the way everlasting." This passage encourages believers to seek God's guidance in evaluating their hearts and actions, making adjustments to align with His will.

Planning in both golf and the Christian life also involves faith and trust. For a golfer, this means trusting in their preparation, their skills, and the process of improvement. They have faith that their hard work and dedication will lead to success on the course. Similarly, Christians are called to trust in God's plan for their lives and to have faith that He will guide them in the right direction. Proverbs 3:5-6 says, "Trust in the LORD with all thine heart; and lean not unto thine own understanding. In all thy ways acknowledge him, and he shall direct thy paths." This verse encourages believers to place their trust in God and to rely on His wisdom and guidance in their planning.

In conclusion, planning is a critical aspect of both golf and the Christian life, involving strategizing, setting goals, seeking guidance, practicing discipline, setting priorities, persevering, reflecting, and trusting in a higher power. For a golfer, strategizing each shot and creating a detailed plan helps to navigate the course effectively and improve performance. This involves setting goals, being flexible, seeking guidance, practicing discipline, setting priorities, persevering, reflecting, and having faith in their preparation. Similarly, in the Christian life, making plans aligned with God's will is essential for living a life that honors Him and fulfills His purposes. Proverbs 16:9 says, "A man's heart deviseth his way: but the LORD directeth his steps." By committing to thoughtful planning in their respective pursuits, both golfers and Christians can achieve their goals, grow in their skills and faith, and fulfill their potential. Planning is a journey marked by continuous effort, dedication, and a commitment to growth, leading to success and fulfillment in both golf and the Christian life.

Chapter 12 Pride

Pride is a significant concept in both golf and the Christian life, and learning to manage it is crucial for personal growth and humility. For a golfer, overcoming pride after a good shot is essential to maintain focus and consistency throughout a round. Golf is a sport where moments of brilliance can easily lead to overconfidence and mistakes if not managed properly. When a golfer makes a great shot, it's natural to feel a sense of accomplishment and pride. However, letting that pride take over can lead to complacency, where the golfer may not give the next shot the same level of attention and care. This can result in mistakes and a loss of momentum. Experienced golfers know that while it's important to celebrate small victories, they must stay humble and focused on the task at hand to maintain their performance. They remind themselves that golf is an unpredictable game and that every shot requires the same level of concentration and effort. Similarly, in the Christian life, avoiding pride in achievements is essential for spiritual growth and maintaining a humble heart. Christians are called to recognize that their abilities and successes are gifts from God and not solely their own doing. Proverbs 16:18 says, "Pride goeth before destruction, and an haughty spirit before a fall." This verse highlights the dangers of pride and the importance of humility. When Christians allow pride to take root in their hearts, it can lead to arrogance and a sense of self-sufficiency, distancing them from God and others.

In both golf and the Christian life, managing pride involves self-awareness and humility. For a golfer, this means being aware of their emotional responses to success and failure and keeping a balanced perspective. They understand that golf is a game of ups and downs and that humility is key to handling both success and adversity. A golfer might acknowledge a good shot with quiet confidence but then quickly refocus on the next challenge. They resist the urge to boast or become complacent, knowing that pride can lead to a fall. Similarly,

Christians are called to be self-aware and humble, recognizing that their achievements are by God's grace. James 4:6 says, "But he giveth more grace. Wherefore he saith, God resisteth the proud, but giveth grace unto the humble." This verse emphasizes the importance of humility and the grace that God extends to those who are humble. By acknowledging their dependence on God, Christians can maintain a humble attitude and avoid the pitfalls of pride.

Managing pride also involves giving credit to others. For a golfer, this might mean acknowledging the support and advice of their coach, the encouragement of their family, or the camaraderie of their fellow players. They understand that their success is not achieved in isolation and that gratitude and acknowledgment of others' contributions are important. Similarly, Christians are called to recognize the support and influence of others in their lives. This might involve thanking mentors, friends, family, and the church community for their encouragement and guidance. Philippians 2:3 says, "Let nothing be done through strife or vainglory; but in lowliness of mind let each esteem other better than themselves." This verse encourages believers to value others above themselves and to acknowledge the contributions of others with humility and gratitude.

In both golf and the Christian life, managing pride also involves continuous learning and growth. For a golfer, this means always seeking to improve and recognizing that there is always more to learn. They stay open to feedback and remain teachable, understanding that pride can hinder their development. This attitude of continuous improvement helps golfers stay grounded and focused on their long-term goals rather than becoming complacent after a good performance. Similarly, Christians are called to continually seek spiritual growth and to remain teachable. Proverbs 11:2 says, "When pride cometh, then cometh shame: but with the lowly is wisdom." This verse highlights the relationship between humility and wisdom, encouraging believers to stay humble and open to learning. By recognizing that there is always room for growth, Christians can avoid the trap of pride and continue to develop their faith.

Another important aspect of managing pride is service to others. For a golfer, this might mean mentoring younger players, sharing their knowledge and experience, and contributing to the golfing community. Acts of service help golfers stay humble and focused on the well-being of others rather than solely on their own achievements. Similarly, Christians are called to serve others as a way of demonstrating humility and gratitude. Serving others shifts the focus away from oneself and fosters a spirit of humility and compassion. Galatians 5:13 says, "For, brethren, ye have been called unto liberty; only use not liberty for an occasion to the flesh, but by love serve one another." This verse encourages believers to use their freedom to serve others in love, helping them stay humble and connected to their community.

In both golf and the Christian life, managing pride also involves acknowledging and learning from mistakes. For a golfer, this means being honest about their performance, analyzing their mistakes, and using them as opportunities for growth. They understand that everyone makes mistakes and that humility allows them to learn and improve. This attitude helps golfers stay focused on their development rather than being weighed down by pride or shame. Similarly, Christians are called to acknowledge their shortcomings and seek God's forgiveness and guidance. 1 John 1:9 says, "If we confess our sins, he is faithful and just to forgive us our sins, and to cleanse us from all unrighteousness." This verse emphasizes the importance of confession and humility in the Christian life. By acknowledging their mistakes and seeking God's forgiveness, believers can maintain a humble heart and continue to grow spiritually.

In both golf and the Christian life, managing pride involves maintaining a sense of perspective. For a golfer, this means recognizing that golf is just one aspect of their life and that their worth is not solely determined by their performance on the course. They keep a balanced perspective, understanding that their identity and value are not defined by their successes or failures in golf. This perspective helps golfers stay grounded and humble, allowing them to enjoy the game without becoming consumed by pride. Similarly, Christians are called to maintain a perspective that values their relationship with God above all else. They understand that their worth is found in being children of God and that their achievements are secondary to their identity in Christ. Romans 12:3 says, "For I say, through the grace given unto me, to every man that is among you, not to think of himself more highly than he ought to think; but to think soberly, according as God hath dealt to every man the measure of faith." This verse encourages believers to maintain a humble perspective and to recognize their value in God's eyes.

In conclusion, managing pride is a crucial aspect of both golf and the Christian life, involving self-awareness, humility, giving credit to others, continuous learning, service, acknowledging mistakes, and maintaining perspective. For a golfer, overcoming pride after a good shot involves staying humble, focused, and grounded, recognizing the contributions of others, and continually seeking to improve. This helps golfers maintain consistency and avoid the pitfalls of overconfidence. Similarly, in the Christian life, avoiding pride in achievements involves recognizing that all abilities and successes are gifts from God, maintaining humility, valuing others, serving, acknowledging mistakes, and keeping a perspective that honors God. Proverbs 16:18 says, "Pride goeth before destruction, and an haughty spirit before a fall." By committing to humility and managing pride, both golfers and Christians can achieve their goals, grow in their skills and faith, and live lives that honor God and reflect His love and grace. Managing pride is a journey marked by continuous effort, self-reflection, and a commitment to humility, leading to success and fulfillment in both golf and the Christian life.

Chapter 13 Pressure Situations

Pressure situations are an inevitable part of both golf and the Christian life, requiring the ability to stay calm, focused, and trust in one's abilities or faith to navigate high-stress moments effectively. For a golfer, handling high-stress moments is crucial for maintaining performance and achieving success. Golf is a sport that demands precision and concentration, and the pressure can be intense, especially during critical shots in a tournament or when trying to make a crucial putt. Golfers often find themselves in situations where the stakes are high, and the outcome of a single shot can determine their overall performance. In these moments, it's essential for golfers to manage their stress, maintain their composure, and stay focused on their game. Techniques such as deep breathing, visualization, and positive self-talk are commonly used to calm nerves and enhance concentration. Experienced golfers know that staying relaxed and focused helps them execute their shots with precision and confidence. They also understand the importance of maintaining a positive mindset and not letting the pressure of the situation overwhelm them. This mental resilience is developed through practice, experience, and a consistent approach to handling stress. Similarly, in the Christian life, trusting God in stressful times is crucial for maintaining peace and resilience. Christians often face pressure situations in various aspects of their lives, such as work, relationships, health, and finances. In these moments, trusting in God's strength and guidance is essential for navigating challenges and finding peace amidst stress. Philippians 4:13 says, "I can do all things through Christ which strengtheneth me." This verse reminds believers that they can rely on Christ's strength to handle any situation and that their faith provides the support and resilience needed to overcome challenges.

In both golf and the Christian life, handling pressure situations involves preparation and mental readiness. For a golfer, this means practicing under pressure conditions to simulate high-stress scenarios. They might play practice rounds with specific challenges or compete in smaller tournaments to build their ability to handle stress. This preparation helps golfers become familiar with the feelings of pressure and learn how to manage them effectively. By practicing under pressure, golfers can develop the mental toughness needed to perform well in actual high-stress situations. Similarly, Christians are encouraged to prepare for stressful times by building a strong foundation of faith. Regular prayer, Bible study, and fellowship with other believers help strengthen their relationship with God and their trust in His promises. By cultivating a deep and resilient faith, Christians can face pressure situations with confidence, knowing that God is with them and will provide the strength they need.

Handling pressure situations also involves staying focused on the present moment. For a golfer, this means concentrating on the current shot rather than worrying about the outcome or dwelling on past mistakes. Staying present helps golfers maintain their focus and execute their shots with precision. They use techniques such as focusing on their breathing, visualizing successful shots, and repeating positive affirmations to stay grounded in the present moment. This focus helps golfers manage stress and perform at their best, regardless of the external pressure. Similarly, Christians are encouraged to stay focused on the present and trust God with their worries and fears. Matthew 6:34 says, "Take therefore no thought for the morrow: for the morrow shall take thought for the things of itself. Sufficient unto the day is the evil thereof." This verse reminds believers to focus on today and not be overwhelmed by concerns about the future. By staying present and trusting God, Christians can handle pressure situations with a calm and focused mind.

In both golf and the Christian life, handling pressure situations also involves maintaining a positive mindset. For a golfer, this means staying optimistic and confident, even in challenging circumstances.

They remind themselves of their strengths and past successes, using positive self-talk to boost their confidence. This positive mindset helps golfers stay motivated and resilient, enabling them to handle pressure with composure. Similarly, Christians are encouraged to maintain a positive mindset by trusting in God's promises and relying on His strength. Romans 8:28 says, "And we know that all things work together for good to them that love God, to them who are the called according to his purpose." This verse reassures believers that God is working for their good, even in difficult situations. By focusing on God's faithfulness and trusting in His plan, Christians can maintain a positive outlook and handle stress with confidence.

Another important aspect of handling pressure situations is having a support system. For a golfer, this might mean having a coach, caddie, or supportive friends and family who provide encouragement and guidance. A strong support system helps golfers feel more confident and less isolated during high-stress moments. They can lean on their support network for advice, motivation, and reassurance. Similarly, Christians are called to support one another in times of stress. Ecclesiastes 4:9-10 says, "Two are better than one; because they have a good reward for their labour. For if they fall, the one will lift up his fellow: but woe to him that is alone when he falleth; for he hath not another to help him up." This passage emphasizes the importance of community and mutual support. By surrounding themselves with fellow believers who can offer encouragement and prayer, Christians can handle pressure situations more effectively.

Handling pressure situations also involves resilience and the ability to bounce back from setbacks. For a golfer, this means not letting a bad shot or a tough hole affect the rest of their game. They learn to quickly recover from mistakes, refocus, and continue playing to the best of their ability. This resilience is developed through practice and experience, as golfers learn to handle pressure and stay calm under stress. Similarly, Christians are called to be resilient in their faith, trusting that God is with them in every situation and that He will help them overcome challenges. James 1:2-4 says, "My brethren, count it all joy when ye fall into divers temptations; knowing this, that the trying of your faith worketh patience. But let patience have her perfect work, that ye may be perfect and entire, wanting nothing." This passage encourages believers to see trials as opportunities for growth and to develop resilience through perseverance.

In both golf and the Christian life, handling pressure situations also involves perspective. For a golfer, this means keeping a balanced view of the game and understanding that one shot or one round does not define their entire golfing career. They maintain perspective by focusing on their long-term goals and not getting overly stressed by immediate outcomes. This balanced perspective helps golfers manage pressure and stay motivated to improve. Similarly, Christians are encouraged to maintain an eternal perspective, recognizing that their current trials are temporary and that their ultimate hope is in Christ. 2 Corinthians 4:17-18 says, "For our light affliction, which is but for a moment, worketh for us a far more exceeding and eternal weight of glory; While we look not at the things which are seen, but at the things which are not seen: for the things which are seen are temporal; but the things which are not seen are eternal." This passage encourages believers to focus on the eternal rewards and to trust that their present challenges are part of God's greater plan.

In conclusion, handling pressure situations is a crucial aspect of both golf and the Christian life, involving preparation, mental readiness, staying focused on the present, maintaining a positive mindset, having a support system, resilience, and perspective. For a golfer, handling high-stress moments involves practicing under pressure, staying focused on the present shot, maintaining a positive mindset, leaning on a support system, being resilient, and keeping a balanced perspective. These strategies help golfers manage stress and perform at their best in critical situations. Similarly, in the Christian life, trusting God in stressful times involves building a strong foundation of faith, staying present and trusting God with worries, maintaining a positive outlook by focusing on God's promises, leaning on a supportive faith community, being resilient through trials, and maintaining an eternal perspective. Philippians 4:13 says, "I can do all things through Christ which strengtheneth me." By committing to these principles, both golfers and Christians can handle pressure situations effectively, achieve their goals, and grow in their skills and faith. Handling pressure is a journey marked by continuous effort, mental and spiritual resilience, and a commitment to trust in one's abilities or faith, leading to success and fulfillment in both golf and the Christian life.

Chapter 14 Positivity

Positivity is a fundamental trait in both golf and the Christian life, serving as a powerful tool to navigate challenges, maintain motivation, and achieve long-term success and fulfillment. For a golfer, staying positive after a bad shot is crucial for maintaining focus and performance throughout a round. Golf is a mentally demanding sport that requires players to stay calm and composed, even when things don't go as planned. A bad shot can be frustrating, but a positive mindset helps golfers to quickly move past it, refocus on the next shot, and avoid letting one mistake affect their entire game. This mental resilience is built through practice, experience, and a conscious effort to maintain a positive attitude. Golfers often use techniques such as positive self-talk, visualization of successful shots, and deep breathing to stay calm and optimistic. By focusing on what they can control and viewing mistakes as opportunities for learning, golfers can keep their confidence and composure, which is essential for performing well under pressure. Similarly, in the Christian life, maintaining a positive outlook is crucial for facing life's challenges with grace and faith. Christians are encouraged to focus on the good, trust in God's plan, and find joy in all circumstances. Philippians 4:8 says, "Finally, brethren, whatsoever things are true, whatsoever things are honest, whatsoever things are just, whatsoever things are pure, whatsoever things are lovely, whatsoever things are of good report; if there be any virtue, and if there be any praise, think on these things." This verse emphasizes the importance of dwelling on positive and virtuous thoughts, which helps believers maintain a positive attitude and strong faith.

In both golf and the Christian life, positivity involves choosing to focus on the positives rather than dwelling on the negatives. For a golfer, this means acknowledging a bad shot but quickly shifting their focus to the next opportunity. They remind themselves of their strengths, past successes, and the enjoyment of the game. This shift in focus helps them to stay motivated and prevent one bad shot from ruining their entire round. Similarly, Christians are encouraged to focus on the blessings and positive aspects of their lives, even in the midst of difficulties. By recognizing God's goodness, remembering His faithfulness, and counting their blessings, believers can maintain a positive outlook and trust that God is working for their good. Romans 8:28 says, "And we know that all things work together for good to them that love God, to them who are the called according to his purpose." This verse reassures Christians that God is in control and that He can bring good out of every situation.

Positivity also involves the practice of gratitude. For a golfer, this means being thankful for the opportunity to play, the beauty of the course, the support of friends and family, and the joy of the game itself. Gratitude helps golfers keep things in perspective and appreciate the experience, regardless of their performance. Similarly, Christians are called to cultivate an attitude of gratitude, recognizing and giving thanks for God's blessings in their lives. 1 Thessalonians 5:18 says, "In every thing give thanks: for this is the will of God in Christ Jesus concerning you." This verse encourages believers to give thanks in all circumstances, fostering a positive and thankful heart that can withstand life's challenges.

In both golf and the Christian life, positivity is reinforced by surrounding oneself with positive influences. For a golfer, this might mean playing with supportive and encouraging friends, working with a positive and motivating coach, or participating in a community of golfers who uplift each other. Positive influences help reinforce a golfer's positive mindset, providing encouragement, support, and constructive feedback. Similarly, Christians are encouraged to surround themselves with fellow believers who uplift and encourage them in their faith. Hebrews 10:24-25 says, "And let us consider one another to provoke unto love and to good works: Not forsaking the assembling of ourselves together, as the manner of some is; but exhorting one another: and so much the more, as ye see the day approaching." This passage emphasizes the importance of community and mutual encouragement, helping believers to stay positive and strong in their faith.

Positivity also involves resilience and the ability to bounce back from setbacks. For a golfer, this means not letting a bad shot or a poor round define their overall performance or affect their love for the game. They learn to view setbacks as temporary and use them as motivation to improve. This resilience is developed through experience and a commitment to maintaining a positive attitude. Similarly, Christians are called to be resilient in their faith, trusting that God is with them in every situation and that He will help them overcome challenges. James 1:2-4 says, "My brethren, count it all joy when ye fall into divers temptations; knowing this, that the trying of your faith worketh patience. But let patience have her perfect work, that ye may be perfect and entire, wanting nothing." This passage encourages believers to see trials as opportunities for growth and to develop resilience through perseverance and a positive attitude.

In both golf and the Christian life, positivity also involves looking forward with hope and expectation. For a golfer, this means setting goals, visualizing success, and staying optimistic about their potential and future performance. They focus on the progress they are making and the improvements they have achieved, using this positive outlook to fuel their motivation and determination. Similarly, Christians are encouraged to look forward with hope, trusting in God's promises and having a positive expectation for the future. Jeremiah 29:11 says, "For I know the thoughts that I think toward you, saith the LORD, thoughts of peace, and not of evil, to give you an expected end." This verse reassures believers that God has good plans for their future, fostering a sense of hope and positivity.

Another important aspect of positivity is the impact it has on others. For a golfer, maintaining a positive attitude can influence their playing partners and create a more enjoyable and supportive atmosphere on the course. Positivity can be contagious, uplifting others and fostering a sense of camaraderie and encouragement. Similarly, Christians are called to be a positive influence on those around them, reflecting God's love and grace in their interactions. Matthew 5:16 says, "Let your light so shine before men, that they may see your good works, and glorify your Father which is in heaven." This verse encourages believers to let their positivity and good works shine, bringing glory to God and positively impacting others.

In conclusion, positivity is a vital quality in both golf and the Christian life, involving a focus on the positives, the practice of gratitude, surrounding oneself with positive influences, resilience, looking forward with hope, and being a positive influence on others. For a golfer, staying positive after a bad shot involves quickly moving past mistakes, focusing on the next opportunity, practicing gratitude, seeking positive influences, and maintaining resilience. This positive mindset helps golfers perform better, enjoy the game, and stay motivated. Similarly, in the Christian life, maintaining a positive outlook involves focusing on God's goodness, practicing gratitude, surrounding oneself with encouraging believers, being resilient in faith, looking forward with hope, and positively impacting others. Philippians 4:8 says, "Finally, brethren, whatsoever things are true, whatsoever things are honest, whatsoever things are just, whatsoever things are pure, whatsoever things are lovely, whatsoever things are of good report; if there be any virtue, and if there be any praise, think on these things." By committing to positivity in their respective pursuits, both golfers and Christians can navigate challenges effectively, achieve their goals, and experience greater joy and fulfillment. Positivity is a journey marked by continuous effort, gratitude, resilience, and a commitment to maintaining a positive attitude, leading to success and satisfaction in both golf and the Christian life.

Chapter 15 Precision in Putting

Precision in putting is crucial for golfers, just as precision in following God's word is essential for Christians. For a golfer, accurate putting can make the difference between a good score and a frustrating round. Putting requires a combination of skill, focus, and precision. The golfer must read the greens, considering the slope, grain, and speed of the grass. They must align their putt accurately and control the force and direction with which they strike the ball. Even the slightest misjudgment can result in a missed putt, turning a potential birdie into a bogey. To achieve precision in putting, golfers practice diligently, often spending hours on the putting green to develop their touch and consistency. They learn to stay calm and focused, blocking out distractions and concentrating on the task at hand. This meticulous attention to detail is what allows top golfers to consistently make putts under pressure, demonstrating the importance of precision in their game. Similarly, in the Christian life, precision in following God's word is paramount. Christians are called to live their lives in a way that is pleasing to God, adhering closely to His teachings and commandments. This requires a deep understanding of the Bible, as well as a commitment to applying its principles in daily life. Psalm 19:14 says, "Let the words of my mouth, and the meditation of my heart, be acceptable in thy sight, O LORD, my strength, and my redeemer." This verse highlights the importance of aligning one's thoughts, words, and actions with God's will, striving for a life that reflects His love and truth.

In both golf and the Christian life, precision involves careful attention to detail. For a golfer, this means paying close attention to the nuances of the greens, the position of the ball, and the mechanics of their stroke. They must be precise in their alignment, stance, grip, and follow-through to ensure that the ball travels accurately towards the hole. This level of precision is developed through consistent practice and a disciplined approach to the game. Similarly, Christians are called to pay close attention to the details of their faith, ensuring that their beliefs and actions are in line with God's word. This involves studying the Bible regularly, praying for wisdom and guidance, and seeking to understand and apply its teachings in every aspect of life. By focusing on the details, believers can live a life that is pleasing to God and reflects His truth.

Precision also involves consistency. For a golfer, being precise in putting means consistently executing the same stroke with accuracy and control. This consistency comes from repeated practice and a deep understanding of their technique. Golfers work on developing a reliable putting routine, one that they can replicate under various conditions and pressures. This routine helps them maintain their focus and precision, even when the stakes are high. Similarly, Christians are called to be consistent in their faith, striving to follow God's word with precision in every situation. This means consistently living out their values, making decisions that honor God, and reflecting His love and truth in their interactions with others. By being consistent in their faith, believers can build a strong and reliable foundation that guides them through life's challenges.

In both golf and the Christian life, precision also involves self-discipline. For a golfer, this means having the self-discipline to practice regularly, to stay focused during rounds, and to maintain a positive attitude even when things don't go as planned. Precision in putting requires a disciplined approach to training, a commitment to improving one's skills, and the mental toughness to stay calm under pressure. Similarly, Christians are called to exercise self-discipline in their spiritual lives, committing to regular prayer, Bible study, and worship. Self-discipline helps believers stay focused on their faith, resist temptations, and maintain a strong relationship with God. Galatians 5:22-23 says, "But the fruit of the Spirit is love, joy, peace, longsuffering, gentleness, goodness, faith, Meekness, temperance:

against such there is no law." This passage highlights the importance of self-discipline (temperance) as a fruit of the Spirit, essential for living a life that honors God.

Precision in both golf and the Christian life also involves humility. For a golfer, humility means recognizing that there is always room for improvement and being open to learning and feedback. It involves acknowledging mistakes, learning from them, and striving to do better. Humility helps golfers stay grounded and focused on their development, rather than becoming complacent or overly confident. Similarly, Christians are called to live with humility, recognizing their dependence on God and their need for His guidance and grace. James 4:10 says, "Humble yourselves in the sight of the Lord, and he shall lift you up." This verse emphasizes the importance of humility in the Christian life, encouraging believers to rely on God and seek His help in their journey of faith.

Another important aspect of precision is intentionality. For a golfer, being precise in putting means being intentional with every aspect of their stroke, from the setup to the execution. They take the time to carefully line up their putt, visualize the path of the ball, and execute their stroke with purpose and focus. This intentionality helps them achieve greater accuracy and consistency in their putting. Similarly, Christians are called to live with intentionality, making deliberate choices that reflect their commitment to God and His word. This means being intentional in their relationships, their work, and their daily decisions, striving to honor God in all they do. Colossians 3:17 says, "And whatsoever ye do in word or deed, do all in the name of the Lord Jesus, giving thanks to God and the Father by him." This verse encourages believers to be intentional in their actions, doing everything for the glory of God.

Precision in both golf and the Christian life also involves perseverance. For a golfer, achieving precision in putting requires perseverance and a willingness to keep practicing and improving, even when progress is slow. It means not giving up after a few bad putts but continuing to work on their skills and strive for better results. Perseverance helps golfers stay committed to their goals and maintain their focus, even in the face of challenges. Similarly, Christians are called to persevere in their faith, continuing to follow God's word and seek His guidance, even when the journey is difficult. Romans 5:3-4 says, "And not only so, but we glory in tribulations also: knowing that tribulation worketh patience; And patience, experience; and experience, hope." This passage encourages believers to persevere through trials, trusting that their perseverance will lead to spiritual growth and hope.

Precision also involves trust. For a golfer, this means trusting in their training, their technique, and their ability to execute their putt. They trust that their practice and preparation will pay off, and they approach each putt with confidence. Similarly, Christians are called to trust in God's word and His promises, relying on His guidance and strength to live a life that honors Him. Proverbs 3:5-6 says, "Trust in the LORD with all thine heart; and lean not unto thine own understanding. In all thy ways acknowledge him, and he shall direct thy paths." This verse encourages believers to trust in God and follow His direction, knowing that He will guide them with precision and care.

In both golf and the Christian life, precision is also about integrity. For a golfer, this means playing the game with honesty and fairness, adhering to the rules and respecting the spirit of the game. Precision in putting requires golfers to be truthful about their performance and to strive for improvement with integrity. Similarly, Christians are called to live with integrity, following God's word with honesty and sincerity. Psalm 25:21 says, "Let integrity and uprightness preserve me; for I wait on thee." This verse highlights the importance of integrity in the Christian life, encouraging believers to uphold their values and live truthfully.

In conclusion, precision is a vital quality in both golf and the Christian life, involving careful attention to detail, consistency, self-discipline, humility, intentionality, perseverance, trust, and integrity. For a golfer, precision in putting means paying close attention to the details of their stroke, practicing consistently, maintaining self-discipline, staying humble, being intentional, persevering through challenges, trusting in their training, and playing with integrity. This precision helps golfers achieve better accuracy, consistency, and overall performance in their game. Similarly, in the Christian life, precision in following God's word involves studying the Bible, applying its teachings with care, practicing self-discipline, living with humility, making intentional choices, persevering in faith, trusting in God's guidance, and living with integrity. Psalm 19:14 says, "Let the words of my mouth, and the meditation of my heart, be acceptable in thy sight, O LORD, my strength, and my redeemer." By committing to precision in their respective pursuits, both golfers and Christians can achieve their goals, grow in their skills and faith, and live lives that honor God. Precision is a journey marked by continuous effort, attention to detail, and a commitment to excellence, leading to success and fulfillment in both golf and the Christian life.

Chapter 16 Patience in Adversity

Patience in adversity is a crucial quality for both golfers and Christians, as it allows them to remain calm, focused, and resilient in the face of challenges and setbacks. For a golfer, patience during a tough round is essential for maintaining composure and performing well despite difficulties. Golf is a sport that can be incredibly frustrating, with unpredictable elements like weather, course conditions, and even bad luck affecting a player's performance. When a golfer faces a challenging round, where shots aren't going as planned or the ball keeps landing in difficult spots, it's easy to become frustrated and lose focus. However, a patient golfer understands the importance of staying calm and not letting a few bad shots ruin the entire round. They take each shot one at a time, focusing on what they can control and not dwelling on mistakes. This patience helps them to avoid compounding errors and allows them to recover from setbacks more effectively. They remind themselves that every round has its ups and downs, and maintaining a positive and patient mindset can help turn things around. Similarly, in the Christian life, patience during life's adversities is essential for maintaining faith and finding peace in difficult times. Christians are often faced with trials and tribulations that test their faith and resilience. Whether it's health issues, financial struggles, relationship problems, or other challenges, patience allows believers to trust in God's plan and timing. Romans 12:12 says, "Rejoicing in hope; patient in tribulation; continuing instant in prayer." This verse encourages Christians to remain hopeful, patient in their trials, and steadfast in prayer, knowing that God is with them and will provide strength and guidance.

In both golf and the Christian life, patience involves maintaining a long-term perspective. For a golfer, this means understanding that one bad round or a series of poor shots does not define their overall ability or potential. They recognize that improvement takes time and that patience is key to developing their skills and achieving their goals. By keeping a long-term perspective, golfers can stay motivated and focused on their practice and development, even when immediate results are disappointing. Similarly, Christians are encouraged to maintain a long-term perspective on their faith journey, trusting that God is working in their lives even when they can't see immediate results. James 1:3-4 says, "Knowing this, that the trying of your faith worketh patience. But let patience have her perfect work, that ye may be perfect and entire, wanting nothing." This passage reminds believers that trials and tribulations help to develop patience and maturity, leading to spiritual growth and completeness.

Patience in adversity also involves emotional regulation. For a golfer, this means managing their emotions during a tough round, staying calm and composed rather than getting angry or discouraged. Emotional regulation helps golfers to think clearly and make better decisions on the course, rather than acting impulsively out of frustration. Techniques such as deep breathing, visualization, and positive self-talk can help golfers to stay calm and maintain their patience. Similarly, Christians are called to manage their emotions during life's adversities, trusting in God's peace and strength to carry them through. Philippians 4:6-7 says, "Be careful for nothing; but in every thing by prayer and supplication with thanksgiving let your requests be made known unto God. And the peace of God, which passeth all understanding, shall keep your hearts and minds through Christ Jesus." This verse encourages believers to turn to God in prayer, trusting that His peace will guard their hearts and minds, helping them to stay patient and calm in the face of challenges.

Another important aspect of patience in adversity is perseverance. For a golfer, this means continuing to play their best, even when the round is not going well. They don't give up or lose motivation, but instead, they keep trying and focusing on each shot. Perseverance helps golfers to stay committed to their game and to keep improving, even when progress seems slow or setbacks occur. Similarly, Christians are called to persevere in their faith, continuing to trust in God and follow His guidance, even when faced with trials. Galatians 6:9 says, "And let us not be weary in well doing: for in due season we shall reap, if we faint not." This verse encourages believers to keep doing good and to persevere, trusting that their efforts will bear fruit in God's perfect timing.

Patience in adversity also involves seeking support and encouragement. For a golfer, this might mean leaning on their coach, caddie, or fellow players for advice and encouragement during a tough round. A supportive community can provide valuable insights, motivation, and reassurance, helping golfers to stay patient and focused. Similarly, Christians are encouraged to seek support and encouragement from their faith community during times of adversity. Hebrews 10:24-25 says, "And let us consider one another to provoke unto love and to good works: Not forsaking the assembling of ourselves together, as the manner of some is; but exhorting one another: and so much the more, as ye see the day approaching." This passage emphasizes the importance of community and mutual encouragement, helping believers to stay strong and patient in their faith.

In both golf and the Christian life, patience in adversity also involves learning and growth. For a golfer, tough rounds and challenging situations provide opportunities for learning and improvement. By analyzing their performance, understanding their mistakes, and making adjustments, golfers can grow and develop their skills. This mindset helps them to view adversity as a valuable part of their journey, rather than just a setback. Similarly, Christians are called to see adversities as opportunities for spiritual growth and deepening their faith. Romans 5:3-4 says, "And not only so, but we glory in tribulations also: knowing that tribulation worketh patience; And patience, experience; and experience, hope." This passage encourages believers to rejoice in their trials, knowing that they produce patience, character, and hope.

Patience in adversity also involves trusting in God's timing and plan. For a golfer, this means trusting that their hard work and practice will eventually pay off, even if they don't see immediate results. They trust in the process and stay committed to their goals, believing that their patience and perseverance will lead to success. Similarly, Christians are called to trust in God's timing and plan for their lives, even when it doesn't align with their own expectations. Proverbs 3:5-6 says, "Trust in the LORD with all thine heart; and lean not unto thine own understanding. In all thy ways acknowledge him, and he shall direct thy paths." This verse encourages believers to trust in God and rely on His wisdom and guidance, knowing that He will lead them on the right path.

In both golf and the Christian life, patience in adversity also involves maintaining hope and optimism. For a golfer, this means staying hopeful and positive, even when facing difficult rounds or setbacks. They remind themselves of their goals, their love for the game, and the progress they have made, using these positive thoughts to stay motivated and patient. Similarly, Christians are encouraged to maintain hope and optimism, trusting in God's promises and His faithfulness. Romans 12:12 says, "Rejoicing in hope; patient in tribulation; continuing instant in prayer." This verse emphasizes the importance of rejoicing in hope, being patient in trials, and remaining steadfast in prayer, helping believers to stay positive and resilient in the face of adversity.

In conclusion, patience in adversity is a vital quality for both golfers and Christians, involving maintaining a long-term perspective, emotional regulation, perseverance, seeking support, learning and growth, trusting in God's timing, and maintaining hope and optimism. For a golfer, patience during a tough round means staying calm, focused, and motivated, even when faced with challenges and setbacks.

This patience helps golfers to perform better, recover from mistakes, and continue improving their skills. Similarly, in the Christian life, patience during life's adversities involves trusting in God's plan, maintaining a positive outlook, seeking support from the faith community, and viewing trials as opportunities for growth. Romans 12:12 says, "Rejoicing in hope; patient in tribulation; continuing instant in prayer." By committing to patience in their respective pursuits, both golfers and Christians can navigate challenges effectively, achieve their goals, and grow in their skills and faith. Patience in adversity is a journey marked by continuous effort, emotional and spiritual resilience, and a commitment to maintaining a positive and trusting attitude, leading to success and fulfillment in both golf and the Christian life.

Chapter 17 Peace of Mind

Peace of mind is an essential quality for both golfers and Christians, as it allows them to remain calm, focused, and centered amidst the challenges they face. For a golfer, staying calm and focused is crucial for maintaining performance and enjoying the game. Golf is a sport that requires a high level of concentration and mental stability. When a golfer faces difficult shots, challenging weather conditions, or the pressure of a competitive round, it's easy to become anxious or distracted. However, a golfer who can maintain peace of mind can approach each shot with clarity and confidence. Techniques such as deep breathing, visualization, and positive self-talk help golfers stay calm and focused. By visualizing successful shots and taking deep breaths to relax, they can reduce stress and maintain a steady rhythm. This calm mindset allows golfers to make better decisions and execute their shots more effectively. Additionally, staying focused helps golfers block out distractions and stay present in the moment, which is essential for maintaining consistency and achieving good scores. Similarly, in the Christian life, finding peace in God is essential for navigating life's challenges with grace and faith. Christians are called to trust in God's presence and promises, finding peace in the assurance that He is with them and in control of their circumstances. John 14:27 says, "Peace I leave with you, my peace I give unto you: not as the world giveth, give I unto you. Let not your heart be troubled, neither let it be afraid." This verse highlights the unique and profound peace that Jesus offers to His followers, a peace that surpasses worldly understanding and alleviates fear and anxiety.

In both golf and the Christian life, peace of mind involves letting go of worries and focusing on what can be controlled. For a golfer, this means accepting that not every shot will be perfect and that external factors like weather or course conditions are beyond their control. They focus on their technique, their strategy, and their mindset, trusting that their preparation and practice will guide them through the round. By letting go of perfectionism and embracing a calm, focused approach, golfers can enjoy the game more and perform better under pressure. Similarly, Christians are encouraged to let go of worries and trust in God's sovereignty. Philippians 4:6-7 says, "Be careful for nothing; but in every thing by prayer and supplication with thanksgiving let your requests be made known unto God. And the peace of God, which passeth all understanding, shall keep your hearts and minds through Christ Jesus." This passage encourages believers to present their concerns to God in prayer, trusting that His peace will guard their hearts and minds, allowing them to remain calm and focused on His promises.

Peace of mind also involves maintaining a positive outlook. For a golfer, staying positive helps them to recover from bad shots and keep their confidence intact. They remind themselves of their strengths and past successes, using positive self-talk to boost their morale. This positive mindset helps golfers stay motivated and resilient, enabling them to handle the ups and downs of the game with grace. Similarly, Christians are called to maintain a positive outlook by focusing on God's goodness and faithfulness. Philippians 4:8 says, "Finally, brethren, whatsoever things are true, whatsoever things are honest, whatsoever things are just, whatsoever things are pure, whatsoever things are lovely, whatsoever things are of good report; if there be any virtue, and if there be any praise, think on these things." This verse encourages believers to dwell on positive and virtuous thoughts, which helps to cultivate peace and joy in their hearts.

In both golf and the Christian life, peace of mind also involves cultivating a sense of gratitude. For a golfer, being grateful for the opportunity to play, the beauty of the course, and the camaraderie with fellow players helps to create a positive and peaceful mindset. Gratitude helps golfers appreciate the experience, regardless of their performance, and keeps them grounded in the joy of the game. Similarly, Christians are encouraged to cultivate gratitude by recognizing and giving thanks for God's blessings in their lives. 1 Thessalonians 5:18 says, "In every thing give thanks: for this is the will of God in Christ Jesus concerning you." This verse highlights the importance of gratitude in the Christian life, encouraging believers to give thanks in all circumstances, which fosters a sense of peace and contentment.

Peace of mind in both golf and the Christian life also involves practicing mindfulness and staying present. For a golfer, this means focusing on the current shot and not letting their mind wander to past mistakes or future outcomes. Mindfulness helps golfers stay in the moment, fully engaged in their game, and able to respond to challenges with clarity and composure. Techniques such as deep breathing, focusing on the physical sensations of the swing, and visualizing successful shots can help golfers stay present and maintain peace of mind. Similarly, Christians are encouraged to practice mindfulness by focusing on God's presence and trusting Him with their concerns. Matthew 6:34 says, "Take therefore no thought for the morrow: for the morrow shall take thought for the things of itself. Sufficient unto the day is the evil thereof." This verse reminds believers to focus on today and trust God with the future, which helps to reduce anxiety and cultivate peace.

In both golf and the Christian life, peace of mind also involves seeking support and encouragement from others. For a golfer, having a supportive coach, caddie, or fellow players can provide valuable advice, encouragement, and reassurance during a round. A supportive community helps golfers feel more confident and less isolated, allowing them to maintain peace of mind even in challenging situations. Similarly, Christians are called to support and encourage one another, finding strength and peace in the fellowship of other believers. Hebrews 10:24-25 says, "And let us consider one another to provoke unto love and to good works: Not forsaking the assembling of ourselves together, as the manner of some is; but exhorting one another: and so much the more, as ye see the day approaching." This passage emphasizes the importance of community and mutual encouragement, helping believers to stay strong and peaceful in their faith.

Peace of mind in both golf and the Christian life also involves trusting in a higher power. For a golfer, this means trusting in their training, their skills, and their ability to perform under pressure. They rely on their preparation and experience to guide them through challenging rounds, trusting that their hard work will pay off. Similarly, Christians are called to trust in God's power and His plan for their lives. Proverbs 3:5-6 says, "Trust in the LORD with all thine heart; and lean not unto thine own understanding. In all thy ways acknowledge him, and he shall direct thy paths." This verse encourages believers to trust in God and rely on His wisdom and guidance, which helps to cultivate peace of mind and reduce anxiety.

In both golf and the Christian life, peace of mind also involves maintaining a balanced perspective. For a golfer, this means recognizing that golf is just one part of their life and that their worth is not solely determined by their performance on the course. They keep a balanced perspective by enjoying the game, appreciating the process of improvement, and not getting overly stressed by immediate outcomes. This balanced approach helps golfers maintain peace of mind and enjoy the game more fully. Similarly, Christians are encouraged to maintain a balanced perspective by focusing on their relationship with God and recognizing that their worth is found in being children of God. Romans 8:38-39 says, "For I am persuaded, that neither death, nor life, nor angels, nor principalities, nor powers, nor things present, nor things to come, nor height, nor depth, nor any other creature, shall be able to separate us from the love of God, which is in Christ Jesus our Lord." This passage reassures believers of God's unchanging love and encourages them to find peace in their identity as His beloved children.

In conclusion, peace of mind is a vital quality in both golf and the Christian life, involving letting go of worries, maintaining a positive outlook, cultivating gratitude, practicing mindfulness, seeking support, trusting in a higher power, and maintaining a balanced perspective. For a golfer, staying calm and focused means using techniques to stay present, positive, and resilient, which helps them perform better and enjoy the game more. Similarly, in the Christian life, finding peace in God involves trusting in His presence and promises, practicing gratitude, focusing on positive thoughts, seeking support from fellow believers, and maintaining a balanced perspective. John 14:27 says, "Peace I leave with you, my peace I give unto you: not as the world giveth, give I unto you. Let not your heart be troubled, neither let it be afraid." By committing to peace of mind in their respective pursuits, both golfers and Christians can navigate challenges effectively, achieve their goals, and experience greater joy and fulfillment. Peace of mind is a journey marked by continuous effort, trust, gratitude, and a commitment to maintaining a calm and centered attitude, leading to success and satisfaction in both golf and the Christian life.

Chapter 18 Proper Technique

Proper technique is essential for both golfers and Christians, as it leads to better results and a more fulfilling experience in their respective pursuits. For a golfer, using proper technique is crucial for achieving consistency, accuracy, and power in their shots. Golf is a sport that demands precision and control, and even the slightest flaw in technique can lead to poor performance. Proper technique involves various elements, such as the grip, stance, posture, alignment, swing mechanics, and follow-through. Each aspect plays a vital role in ensuring that the golfer can hit the ball accurately and consistently. For example, a correct grip allows for better control of the club, a proper stance provides stability and balance, and a well-executed swing generates power and accuracy. Golfers spend countless hours practicing and refining their technique, often seeking guidance from coaches and using training aids to improve their skills. This dedication to mastering the fundamentals of the game helps them achieve better results on the course and enjoy the game more fully. Similarly, in the Christian life, following proper spiritual disciplines is essential for growing in faith and living a life that honors God. Spiritual disciplines are practices that help believers deepen their relationship with God, develop their character, and align their lives with His will. These disciplines include prayer, Bible study, worship, fasting, fellowship, service, and meditation. Each discipline plays a crucial role in nurturing the believer's spiritual growth and strengthening their faith. 1 Corinthians 9:25 says, "And every man that striveth for the mastery is temperate in all things." This verse highlights the importance of self-discipline and commitment in pursuing excellence, whether in sports or spiritual growth.

In both golf and the Christian life, proper technique involves a commitment to learning and improvement. For a golfer, this means being open to instruction, seeking feedback, and continually refining their skills. They understand that mastering golf requires ongoing practice and a willingness to make adjustments based on their performance. By focusing on proper technique and being disciplined in their practice, golfers can improve their consistency, accuracy, and overall performance. Similarly, Christians are called to be diligent in their spiritual disciplines, continually seeking to grow in their faith and understanding of God's word. This involves regular Bible study, prayer, and participation in worship and fellowship. By committing to these practices, believers can deepen their relationship with God and develop a stronger, more mature faith.

Proper technique also involves attention to detail. For a golfer, this means paying close attention to every aspect of their game, from their grip and stance to their swing and follow-through. They understand that small adjustments can make a significant difference in their performance, and they strive to perfect each element of their technique. This attention to detail helps golfers achieve greater accuracy and consistency in their shots, leading to better results on the course. Similarly, Christians are called to be attentive to the details of their spiritual lives, ensuring that their beliefs and actions align with God's word. This involves studying the Bible carefully, reflecting on its teachings, and applying them to their daily lives. By paying attention to the details of their faith, believers can live in a way that honors God and reflects His love and truth.

In both golf and the Christian life, proper technique involves discipline and consistency. For a golfer, this means practicing regularly and maintaining a disciplined approach to their training. They understand that improvement requires consistent effort and a commitment to mastering the fundamentals of the game. By staying disciplined and focused, golfers can develop the muscle memory and mental toughness needed to perform well under pressure. Similarly, Christians are called to be disciplined in their spiritual practices, committing to regular prayer, Bible study, and worship. Consistency in these disciplines helps believers grow in their faith and develop a deeper relationship with God. Hebrews 12:11 says, "Now no chastening for the present seemeth to be joyous, but grievous: nevertheless afterward it yieldeth the peaceable fruit of righteousness unto them which are exercised thereby." This verse highlights the importance of discipline and the rewards it brings, encouraging believers to stay committed to their spiritual practices.

Proper technique also involves patience and perseverance. For a golfer, mastering proper technique takes time and effort. They understand that improvement doesn't happen overnight and that patience is essential for progress. By persevering through challenges and setbacks, golfers can continue to refine their skills and achieve better results. Similarly, Christians are called to be patient and persevering in their spiritual journey. Developing a strong and mature faith takes time, and believers must be willing to endure trials and challenges. James 1:3-4 says, "Knowing this, that the trying of your faith worketh patience. But let patience have her perfect work, that ye may be perfect and entire, wanting nothing." This passage encourages believers to embrace patience and perseverance, trusting that these qualities will lead to spiritual growth and maturity.

In both golf and the Christian life, proper technique also involves humility. For a golfer, this means being open to learning and recognizing that there is always room for improvement. Humility allows golfers to receive feedback and instruction, which are essential for refining their technique and improving their performance. By staying humble and teachable, golfers can continue to grow and develop their skills. Similarly, Christians are called to live with humility, recognizing their dependence on God and their need for His guidance and grace. James 4:10 says, "Humble yourselves in the sight of the Lord, and he shall lift you up." This verse emphasizes the importance of humility in the Christian life, encouraging believers to rely on God and seek His help in their journey of faith.

Another important aspect of proper technique is intentionality. For a golfer, this means being intentional with every aspect of their game, from their setup to their swing. They take the time to carefully align their shot, visualize the desired outcome, and execute their technique with purpose and focus. This intentionality helps golfers achieve greater accuracy and consistency in their performance. Similarly, Christians are called to live with intentionality, making deliberate choices that reflect their commitment to God and His word. This means being intentional in their relationships, their work, and their daily decisions, striving to honor God in all they do. Colossians 3:17 says, "And whatsoever ye do in word or deed, do all in the name of the Lord Jesus, giving thanks to God and the Father by him." This verse encourages believers to be intentional in their actions, doing everything for the glory of God.

Proper technique in both golf and the Christian life also involves perseverance and resilience. For a golfer, this means continuing to work on their technique, even when faced with challenges or setbacks. They understand that improvement requires perseverance and a willingness to keep trying, even when progress seems slow. By staying resilient and committed to their practice, golfers can overcome obstacles and continue to improve. Similarly, Christians are called to persevere in their faith, continuing to follow God's word and seek His guidance, even when faced with trials. Galatians 6:9 says, "And let us not be weary in well doing: for in due season we shall reap, if we faint not." This verse encourages believers to keep doing good and to persevere, trusting that their efforts will bear fruit in God's perfect timing.

Proper technique also involves trust. For a golfer, this means trusting in their training, their technique, and their ability to execute their shots. They rely on their preparation and practice to guide them through challenging rounds, trusting that their hard work will pay off. Similarly, Christians are called to trust in God's word and His promises, relying on His guidance and strength to live a life that honors Him.

Proverbs 3:5-6 says, "Trust in the LORD with all thine heart; and lean not unto thine own understanding. In all thy ways acknowledge him, and he shall direct thy paths." This verse encourages believers to trust in God and follow His direction, knowing that He will guide them with precision and care.

In both golf and the Christian life, proper technique is also about integrity. For a golfer, this means playing the game with honesty and fairness, adhering to the rules and respecting the spirit of the game. Proper technique requires golfers to be truthful about their performance and to strive for improvement with integrity. Similarly, Christians are called to live with integrity, following God's word with honesty and sincerity. Psalm 25:21 says, "Let integrity and uprightness preserve me; for I wait on thee." This verse highlights the importance of integrity in the Christian life, encouraging believers to uphold their values and live truthfully.

In conclusion, proper technique is a vital quality in both golf and the Christian life, involving a commitment to learning and improvement, attention to detail, discipline and consistency, patience and perseverance, humility, intentionality, trust, and integrity. For a golfer, using proper technique means paying close attention to the details of their game, practicing consistently, staying disciplined, being patient and persevering through challenges, staying humble and teachable, being intentional with their actions, trusting in their training, and playing with integrity. This proper technique helps golfers achieve better accuracy, consistency, and overall performance in their game. Similarly, in the Christian life, following proper spiritual disciplines involves studying the Bible, applying its teachings with care, practicing self-discipline, living with humility, making intentional choices, persevering in faith, trusting in God's guidance, and living with integrity. 1 Corinthians 9:25 says, "And every man that striveth for the mastery is temperate in all things." By committing to proper technique in their respective pursuits, both golfers and Christians can achieve their goals, grow in their skills and faith, and live lives that honor God. Proper technique is a journey marked by continuous effort, attention to detail, and a commitment to excellence, leading to success and fulfillment in both golf and the Christian life.

Chapter 19 Positive Attitude

A positive attitude is essential in both golf and the Christian life, helping individuals stay motivated, resilient, and focused on their goals despite challenges. For a golfer, maintaining a positive attitude throughout the game is crucial for achieving good performance and enjoying the sport. Golf is a challenging and often frustrating game where players face various obstacles, such as difficult course conditions, bad weather, or simply a bad day. It's easy to become discouraged after a missed shot or a bad hole, but a positive attitude can help golfers stay focused and motivated. Instead of dwelling on mistakes, positive golfers focus on what they can control, such as their next shot and their strategy moving forward. They use positive self-talk to boost their confidence and remind themselves of their strengths and past successes. This positive mindset helps golfers to recover quickly from setbacks, maintain their composure, and play to the best of their abilities. Similarly, in the Christian life, keeping a positive attitude is essential for navigating life's ups and downs with faith and hope. Christians are called to maintain a positive outlook, trusting that God is in control and working for their good, even in difficult circumstances. Philippians 2:14 says, "Do all things without murmurings and disputings." This verse encourages believers to approach life with a positive attitude, free from complaining and arguing, which fosters a spirit of contentment and peace.

In both golf and the Christian life, a positive attitude involves focusing on the positives rather than the negatives. For a golfer, this means acknowledging a bad shot but quickly shifting their focus to the next opportunity. They remind themselves of the good shots they've made and the progress they've achieved, using these positive memories to stay motivated and confident. This shift in focus helps golfers to maintain their enthusiasm for the game and to approach each shot with a fresh perspective. Similarly, Christians are encouraged to focus on the blessings and positive aspects of their lives, even in the midst of trials. By recognizing God's goodness, remembering His faithfulness, and counting their blessings, believers can maintain a positive outlook and trust that God is working for their good. Romans 8:28 says, "And we know that all things work together for good to them that love God, to them who are the called according to his purpose." This verse reassures Christians that God is in control and that He can bring good out of every situation.

A positive attitude also involves the practice of gratitude. For a golfer, being grateful for the opportunity to play, the beauty of the course, the camaraderie with fellow players, and the joy of the game itself helps to create a positive and fulfilling experience. Gratitude helps golfers appreciate the sport, regardless of their performance, and keeps them grounded in the joy of playing. Similarly, Christians are called to cultivate an attitude of gratitude, recognizing and giving thanks for God's blessings in their lives. 1 Thessalonians 5:18 says, "In every thing give thanks: for this is the will of God in Christ Jesus concerning you." This verse encourages believers to give thanks in all circumstances, fostering a sense of peace and contentment.

In both golf and the Christian life, a positive attitude is reinforced by surrounding oneself with positive influences. For a golfer, this might mean playing with supportive and encouraging friends, working with a positive and motivating coach, or participating in a community of golfers who uplift each other. Positive influences help reinforce a golfer's positive mindset, providing encouragement, support, and constructive feedback. Similarly, Christians are encouraged to surround themselves with fellow believers who uplift and encourage them in their faith. Hebrews 10:24-25 says, "And let us consider one another to provoke unto love and to good works: Not forsaking the assembling of ourselves together, as the manner of some is; but exhorting one another: and so much the more, as ye see the day approaching." This passage emphasizes the importance of community and mutual encouragement, helping believers to stay positive and strong in their faith.

A positive attitude also involves resilience and the ability to bounce back from setbacks. For a golfer, this means not letting a bad hole or a poor round define their overall performance or affect their love for the game. They learn to view setbacks as temporary and use them as motivation to improve. This resilience is developed through experience and a commitment to maintaining a positive attitude. Similarly, Christians are called to be resilient in their faith, trusting that God is with them in every situation and that He will help them overcome challenges. James 1:2-4 says, "My brethren, count it all joy when ye fall into divers temptations; knowing this, that the trying of your faith worketh patience. But let patience have her perfect work, that ye may be perfect and entire, wanting nothing." This passage encourages believers to see trials as opportunities for growth and to develop resilience through perseverance and a positive attitude.

In both golf and the Christian life, a positive attitude also involves looking forward with hope and expectation. For a golfer, this means setting goals, visualizing success, and staying optimistic about their potential and future performance. They focus on the progress they are making and the improvements they have achieved, using this positive outlook to fuel their motivation and determination. Similarly, Christians are encouraged to look forward with hope, trusting in God's promises and having a positive expectation for the future. Jeremiah 29:11 says, "For I know the thoughts that I think toward you, saith the LORD, thoughts of peace, and not of evil, to give you an expected end." This verse reassures believers that God has good plans for their future, fostering a sense of hope and positivity.

Another important aspect of a positive attitude is the impact it has on others. For a golfer, maintaining a positive attitude can influence their playing partners and create a more enjoyable and supportive atmosphere on the course. Positivity can be contagious, uplifting others and fostering a sense of camaraderie and encouragement. Similarly, Christians are called to be a positive influence on those around them, reflecting God's love and grace in their interactions. Matthew 5:16 says, "Let your light so shine before men, that they may see your good works, and glorify your Father which is in heaven." This verse encourages believers to let their positivity and good works shine, bringing glory to God and positively impacting others.

In conclusion, a positive attitude is a vital quality in both golf and the Christian life, involving a focus on the positives, the practice of gratitude, surrounding oneself with positive influences, resilience, looking forward with hope, and being a positive influence on others. For a golfer, maintaining a positive attitude throughout the game involves quickly moving past mistakes, focusing on the next opportunity, practicing gratitude, seeking positive influences, and maintaining resilience. This positive mindset helps golfers perform better, enjoy the game, and stay motivated. Similarly, in the Christian life, keeping a positive attitude involves focusing on God's goodness, practicing gratitude, surrounding oneself with encouraging believers, being resilient in faith, looking forward with hope, and positively impacting others. Philippians 2:14 says, "Do all things without murmurings and disputings." By committing to a positive attitude in their respective pursuits, both golfers and Christians can navigate challenges effectively, achieve their goals, and experience greater joy and fulfillment. A positive attitude is a journey marked by continuous effort, gratitude, resilience, and a commitment to maintaining a positive outlook, leading to success and satisfaction in both golf and the Christian life.

Chapter 20 Pressure of Competition

The pressure of competition is a significant aspect in both golf and the Christian life, requiring individuals to remain strong, focused, and resilient. For a golfer, competing against others involves not only showcasing their skills but also handling the intense pressure that comes with tournaments and matches. Golf is a sport where mental strength is as crucial as physical skill. During a competition, a golfer must maintain concentration, manage their emotions, and execute their shots with precision despite the presence of spectators, the high stakes, and the performance of their competitors. This pressure can be overwhelming, causing anxiety and affecting performance if not managed properly. To handle this pressure, golfers often use mental strategies such as visualization, positive self-talk, and mindfulness techniques to stay calm and focused. They remind themselves to take one shot at a time, focusing on their own game rather than being distracted by their competitors. Staying in the present moment helps them to avoid being overwhelmed by the magnitude of the competition. Similarly, in the Christian life, standing firm in faith amidst opposition is essential. Christians often face challenges and opposition in various forms, whether it be social, cultural, or spiritual. These challenges can create immense pressure, testing their faith and commitment to God. 1 Corinthians 16:13 says, "Watch ye, stand fast in the faith, quit you like men, be strong." This verse encourages believers to remain vigilant, stand firm in their faith, act with courage, and be strong in the face of adversity.

In both golf and the Christian life, the pressure of competition involves maintaining focus and determination. For a golfer, this means concentrating on their strategy and execution, blocking out distractions, and staying committed to their game plan. They understand that every shot counts and that maintaining focus throughout the round is key to performing well. This focus helps them to manage the pressure and deliver their best performance, regardless of the competition. Similarly, Christians are called to stay focused on their faith and God's promises, even when faced with opposition. They are encouraged to keep their eyes on Jesus and trust in His guidance, knowing that He is with them in every situation. Hebrews 12:2 says, "Looking unto Jesus the author and finisher of our faith; who for the joy that was set before him endured the cross, despising the shame, and is set down at the right hand of the throne of God." This verse reminds believers to focus on Jesus and draw strength from His example of enduring hardship with faith and perseverance.

The pressure of competition also involves managing emotions. For a golfer, this means staying calm and composed, even when faced with difficult shots or unfavorable conditions. Emotional regulation is crucial for maintaining performance under pressure. Golfers use techniques such as deep breathing, visualization, and positive affirmations to manage their emotions and stay in control. By keeping their emotions in check, they can make clear decisions and execute their shots with confidence. Similarly, Christians are called to manage their emotions and remain steadfast in their faith, even when facing trials. Philippians 4:6-7 says, "Be careful for nothing; but in every thing by prayer and supplication with thanksgiving let your requests be made known unto God. And the peace of God, which passeth all understanding, shall keep your hearts and minds through Christ Jesus." This passage encourages believers to bring their concerns to God in prayer, trusting that His peace will guard their hearts and minds, helping them to stay calm and focused amidst pressure.

Another important aspect of handling the pressure of competition is preparation. For a golfer, this means rigorous training, practicing various shots, and mentally preparing for the competition. They study the course, plan their strategy, and visualize their performance. This thorough preparation helps golfers to feel confident and ready to face the competition. They trust in their practice and preparation, knowing that they have done everything possible to prepare for the challenge.

Similarly, Christians are called to prepare themselves spiritually to face opposition. This involves regular prayer, Bible study, and fellowship with other believers. By grounding themselves in God's word and building a strong spiritual foundation, believers can stand firm in their faith when faced with challenges. Ephesians 6:11 says, "Put on the whole armour of God, that ye may be able to stand against the wiles of the devil." This verse highlights the importance of spiritual preparation, encouraging believers to equip themselves with God's truth and strength.

In both golf and the Christian life, the pressure of competition also involves resilience. For a golfer, resilience means bouncing back from bad shots or tough holes, staying positive, and continuing to play their best. They understand that setbacks are part of the game and that resilience is key to overcoming challenges and achieving success. This resilience is developed through experience, practice, and a positive mindset. Similarly, Christians are called to be resilient in their faith, trusting that God is with them and will help them overcome trials. James 1:2-4 says, "My brethren, count it all joy when ye fall into divers temptations; knowing this, that the trying of your faith worketh patience. But let patience have her perfect work, that ye may be perfect and entire, wanting nothing." This passage encourages believers to see trials as opportunities for growth and to develop resilience through perseverance and faith.

In both golf and the Christian life, the pressure of competition also involves relying on support from others. For a golfer, this might mean leaning on their coach, caddie, or fellow players for advice, encouragement, and support. A strong support system can provide valuable insights, motivation, and reassurance, helping golfers to stay focused and confident under pressure. Similarly, Christians are encouraged to seek support from their faith community, finding strength and encouragement in fellowship with other believers. Hebrews 10:24-25 says, "And let us consider one another to provoke unto love and to good works: Not forsaking the assembling of ourselves together, as the manner of some is; but exhorting one another: and so much the more, as ye see the day approaching." This passage emphasizes the importance of community and mutual encouragement, helping believers to stay strong and positive in their faith.

The pressure of competition in both golf and the Christian life also involves maintaining a long-term perspective. For a golfer, this means understanding that one tournament or round does not define their career. They keep their focus on long-term goals and progress, recognizing that setbacks are part of the journey. This perspective helps them to stay motivated and committed to their development, even when faced with immediate challenges. Similarly, Christians are encouraged to maintain an eternal perspective, trusting that their present trials are temporary and that their ultimate hope is in Christ. 2 Corinthians 4:17-18 says, "For our light affliction, which is but for a moment, worketh for us a far more exceeding and eternal weight of glory; While we look not at the things which are seen, but at the things which are not seen: for the things which are seen are temporal; but the things which are not seen are eternal." This passage encourages believers to focus on the eternal rewards and to trust that their current struggles are part of God's greater plan.

In both golf and the Christian life, the pressure of competition also involves trust. For a golfer, this means trusting in their training, their technique, and their ability to perform under pressure. They rely on their preparation and experience to guide them through challenging rounds, trusting that their hard work will pay off. Similarly, Christians are called to trust in God's power and His plan for their lives. Proverbs 3:5-6 says, "Trust in the LORD with all thine heart; and lean not unto thine own understanding. In all thy ways acknowledge him, and he shall direct thy paths." This verse encourages believers to trust in God and rely on His wisdom and guidance, knowing that He will lead them on the right path.

In conclusion, the pressure of competition is a significant aspect in both golf and the Christian life, involving maintaining focus, managing emotions, thorough preparation, resilience, relying on support, maintaining a long-term perspective, and trust. For a golfer, competing against others involves showcasing their skills, handling intense pressure, and staying focused on their game plan. By maintaining a positive attitude, preparing thoroughly, managing emotions, and relying on support, golfers can handle the pressure of competition and perform at their best. Similarly, in the Christian life, standing firm in faith amidst opposition involves trusting in God's presence and promises, preparing spiritually, managing emotions through prayer, and finding strength in the support of fellow believers. 1 Corinthians 16:13 says, "Watch ye, stand fast in the faith, quit you like men, be strong." By committing to these principles, both golfers and Christians can navigate the pressure of competition effectively, achieve their goals, and grow in their skills and faith. Handling the pressure of competition is a journey marked by continuous effort, resilience, trust, and a commitment to staying focused and strong, leading to success and fulfillment in both golf and the Christian life.

Chapter 21 Partnership

Partnership is a fundamental aspect of both golf and the Christian life, highlighting the importance of working together to achieve common goals and support one another. For a golfer, partnering with a caddie is crucial for navigating the complexities of the game. A caddie is not just someone who carries the golfer's clubs; they are a trusted advisor, strategist, and supporter. The caddie provides valuable insights about the course, helps with club selection, and offers encouragement and motivation. This partnership allows the golfer to focus on their performance, knowing they have someone by their side who understands the intricacies of the game and can offer guidance. A strong golfer-caddie partnership is built on trust, communication, and mutual respect. The caddie must understand the golfer's strengths and weaknesses, their preferred strategies, and how to best support them under pressure. Likewise, the golfer must trust the caddie's judgment and be open to their advice. This collaboration enhances the golfer's ability to make informed decisions, maintain focus, and perform at their best. Similarly, in the Christian life, partnering with fellow believers is essential for spiritual growth and support. Christians are called to work together, encourage one another, and bear each other's burdens. Ecclesiastes 4:9 says, "Two are better than one; because they have a good reward for their labour." This verse emphasizes the benefits of partnership, highlighting how collaboration and mutual support lead to greater success and fulfillment.

In both golf and the Christian life, partnership involves effective communication. For a golfer and their caddie, clear and open communication is key to understanding the challenges of the course and making strategic decisions. They discuss each shot, consider various factors such as wind, distance, and terrain, and agree on the best approach. This dialogue helps the golfer feel confident in their choices and stay focused on their game. Similarly, Christians are encouraged to communicate openly and honestly with one another, sharing their struggles, joys, and insights. This communication fosters a sense of community and trust, allowing believers to support and uplift each other. James 5:16 says, "Confess your faults one to another, and pray one for another, that ye may be healed. The effectual fervent prayer of a righteous man availeth much." This verse highlights the importance of sharing and praying for one another, strengthening the bond between believers.

Partnership also involves mutual support and encouragement. For a golfer, having a caddie who provides constant encouragement and positive reinforcement can make a significant difference in their performance. The caddie helps the golfer stay motivated, maintain a positive mindset, and recover quickly from setbacks. This support is especially crucial during challenging rounds when the pressure is high, and maintaining focus is difficult. Similarly, Christians are called to support and encourage one another in their faith journey. Galatians 6:2 says, "Bear ye one another's burdens, and so fulfil the law of Christ." This verse encourages believers to help each other through difficult times, offering support and comfort. By bearing each other's burdens, Christians can build a strong and supportive community that reflects God's love.

In both golf and the Christian life, partnership also involves accountability. For a golfer, a caddie can provide accountability by helping them stay focused on their goals, reminding them of their strategies, and ensuring they maintain proper technique. This accountability helps the golfer stay disciplined and committed to their game plan, even when faced with challenges. Similarly, Christians are encouraged to hold each other accountable in their spiritual walk. Hebrews 10:24-25 says, "And let us consider one another to provoke unto love and to good works: Not forsaking the assembling of ourselves together, as the manner of some is; but exhorting one another: and so much the more, as ye see the day approaching." This passage emphasizes the importance of encouraging and holding each other accountable, helping believers stay committed to their faith and good works.

Partnership in both golf and the Christian life also involves trust. For a golfer, trusting their caddie's advice and judgment is essential for making confident decisions on the course. This trust is built through experience, communication, and mutual respect. A strong partnership allows the golfer to rely on the caddie's expertise, helping them navigate difficult situations and make informed choices. Similarly, Christians are called to trust one another, knowing that their fellow believers have their best interests at heart. Proverbs 27:17 says, "Iron sharpeneth iron; so a man sharpeneth the countenance of his friend." This verse highlights the importance of mutual trust and support, encouraging believers to help each other grow and strengthen their faith.

Another important aspect of partnership is collaboration. For a golfer and their caddie, collaboration means working together to develop a strategy, analyze the course, and make adjustments as needed. This collaborative effort helps the golfer stay focused and perform at their best. Similarly, Christians are encouraged to collaborate with one another, using their unique gifts and talents to serve God and build up the church. 1 Corinthians 12:12 says, "For as the body is one, and hath many members, and all the members of that one body, being many, are one body: so also is Christ." This verse emphasizes the importance of working together as a unified body, each member contributing to the overall mission and growth of the church.

Partnership in both golf and the Christian life also involves empathy and understanding. For a golfer, a caddie who understands their emotional and mental state can provide the right support and encouragement when needed. This empathy helps the golfer feel understood and supported, enhancing their confidence and performance. Similarly, Christians are called to show empathy and understanding toward one another, being sensitive to each other's needs and emotions. Romans 12:15 says, "Rejoice with them that do rejoice, and weep with them that weep." This verse encourages believers to share in each other's joys and sorrows, fostering a deep sense of community and compassion.

In both golf and the Christian life, partnership also involves learning and growth. For a golfer, working with a knowledgeable caddie can provide valuable insights and lessons that help improve their game. The caddie offers feedback, suggests adjustments, and shares their expertise, contributing to the golfer's development. Similarly, Christians are encouraged to learn from one another, sharing their knowledge, experiences, and insights to help each other grow in faith. Colossians 3:16 says, "Let the word of Christ dwell in you richly in all wisdom; teaching and admonishing one another in psalms and hymns and spiritual songs, singing with grace in your hearts to the Lord." This verse highlights the importance of teaching and encouraging one another, promoting spiritual growth and wisdom.

Partnership also involves commitment and loyalty. For a golfer, having a committed and loyal caddie who is dedicated to their success can provide a sense of stability and trust. This commitment helps the golfer feel supported and confident, knowing that their caddie is fully invested in their performance. Similarly, Christians are called to be committed and loyal to one another, supporting each other through all circumstances. Proverbs 17:17 says, "A friend loveth at all times, and a brother is born for adversity." This verse emphasizes the importance of loyalty and commitment in relationships, encouraging believers to stand by each other through thick and thin.

In both golf and the Christian life, partnership also involves celebrating successes together. For a golfer, sharing the joy of a well-played round or a tournament victory with their caddie strengthens their bond and reinforces their partnership. Celebrating successes together creates positive memories and motivates both the golfer and the caddie to continue striving for excellence. Similarly, Christians are encouraged to celebrate each other's successes and achievements, rejoicing together in God's blessings. Romans 12:15 says, "Rejoice with them that do rejoice, and weep with them that weep." This verse highlights the importance of sharing in each other's joys, fostering a sense of community and mutual support.

In conclusion, partnership is a vital quality in both golf and the Christian life, involving effective communication, mutual support, accountability, trust, collaboration, empathy, learning, commitment, and celebrating successes. For a golfer, partnering with a caddie involves working together to navigate the challenges of the game, providing support, encouragement, and strategic guidance. This partnership helps the golfer stay focused, make informed decisions, and perform at their best. Similarly, in the Christian life, partnering with fellow believers involves supporting one another in faith, sharing insights and encouragement, holding each other accountable, and working together to serve God. Ecclesiastes 4:9 says, "Two are better than one; because they have a good reward for their labour." By committing to partnership in their respective pursuits, both golfers and Christians can achieve their goals, grow in their skills and faith, and experience greater fulfillment and success. Partnership is a journey marked by continuous effort, mutual support, trust, and a commitment to working together, leading to success and satisfaction in both golf and the Christian life.

Chapter 22 Precision in Swing

Precision in swing mechanics is essential for a golfer, just as precision in spiritual actions is crucial for a Christian. For a golfer, achieving precision in their swing mechanics is vital for consistency, accuracy, and power. Golf is a game that requires meticulous attention to detail, as even the smallest flaw in a golfer's swing can result in a poor shot. The golf swing is a complex motion that involves the coordination of multiple body parts, including the grip, stance, posture, backswing, downswing, and follow-through. Each element must be executed with precision to achieve the desired ball flight and distance. For instance, a proper grip ensures control of the club, while a balanced stance provides stability. During the backswing, the golfer must maintain a smooth, controlled motion, storing energy that will be released in the downswing. The downswing requires precise timing and coordination to generate power and direct the ball accurately. Finally, a complete follow-through helps maintain balance and control. Golfers spend countless hours practicing and refining their swing mechanics, often using video analysis and feedback from coaches to identify areas for improvement. This dedication to precision helps golfers improve their performance and enjoy the game more fully. Similarly, in the Christian life, precision in spiritual actions is essential for living a life that honors God. Christians are called to align their words and deeds with God's will, ensuring that their actions reflect their faith and values. Colossians 3:17 says, "And whatsoever ye do in word or deed, do all in the name of the Lord Jesus, giving thanks to God and the Father by him." This verse emphasizes the importance of doing everything with a heart of gratitude and a commitment to honoring God.

In both golf and the Christian life, precision involves a commitment to learning and continuous improvement. For a golfer, this means being open to instruction, seeking feedback, and continually refining their swing mechanics. They understand that mastering the golf swing requires ongoing practice and a willingness to make adjustments based on their performance. By focusing on precision and being disciplined in their practice, golfers can improve their consistency, accuracy, and overall performance. Similarly, Christians are called to be diligent in their spiritual practices, continually seeking to grow in their faith and understanding of God's word. This involves regular prayer, Bible study, worship, and fellowship with other believers. By committing to these practices, believers can deepen their relationship with God and develop a stronger, more mature faith.

Precision also involves attention to detail. For a golfer, this means paying close attention to every aspect of their swing, from their grip and stance to their swing path and follow-through. They understand that small adjustments can make a significant difference in their performance, and they strive to perfect each element of their swing. This attention to detail helps golfers achieve greater accuracy and consistency in their shots, leading to better results on the course. Similarly, Christians are called to be attentive to the details of their spiritual lives, ensuring that their beliefs and actions align with God's word. This involves studying the Bible carefully, reflecting on its teachings, and applying them to their daily lives. By paying attention to the details of their faith, believers can live in a way that honors God and reflects His love and truth.

In both golf and the Christian life, precision involves discipline and consistency. For a golfer, this means practicing regularly and maintaining a disciplined approach to their training. They understand that improvement requires consistent effort and a commitment to mastering the fundamentals of the game. By staying disciplined and focused, golfers can develop the muscle memory and mental toughness needed to perform well under pressure. Similarly, Christians are called to be disciplined in their spiritual practices, committing to regular prayer, Bible study, and worship. Consistency in these disciplines helps believers grow in their faith and develop a deeper relationship with God. Hebrews 12:11 says, "Now no chastening for the present seemeth to be joyous, but grievous: nevertheless afterward it yieldeth the peaceable fruit of righteousness unto them which are exercised thereby." This verse highlights the importance of discipline and the rewards it brings, encouraging believers to stay committed to their spiritual practices.

Precision also involves patience and perseverance. For a golfer, mastering precision in swing mechanics takes time and effort. They understand that improvement doesn't happen overnight and that patience is essential for progress. By persevering through challenges and setbacks, golfers can continue to refine their skills and achieve better results. Similarly, Christians are called to be patient and persevering in their spiritual journey. Developing a strong and mature faith takes time, and believers must be willing to endure trials and challenges. James 1:3-4 says, "Knowing this, that the trying of your faith worketh patience. But let patience have her perfect work, that ye may be perfect and entire, wanting nothing." This passage encourages believers to embrace patience and perseverance, trusting that these qualities will lead to spiritual growth and maturity.

In both golf and the Christian life, precision also involves humility. For a golfer, this means recognizing that there is always room for improvement and being open to learning and feedback. Humility allows golfers to receive instruction and make necessary adjustments, which are essential for refining their swing and improving their performance. By staying humble and teachable, golfers can continue to grow and develop their skills. Similarly, Christians are called to live with humility, recognizing their dependence on God and their need for His guidance and grace. James 4:10 says, "Humble yourselves in the sight of the Lord, and he shall lift you up." This verse emphasizes the importance of humility in the Christian life, encouraging believers to rely on God and seek His help in their journey of faith.

Another important aspect of precision is intentionality. For a golfer, this means being intentional with every aspect of their swing, from their setup to their follow-through. They take the time to carefully align their shot, visualize the desired outcome, and execute their swing with purpose and focus. This intentionality helps golfers achieve greater accuracy and consistency in their performance. Similarly, Christians are called to live with intentionality, making deliberate choices that reflect their commitment to God and His word. This means being intentional in their relationships, their work, and their daily decisions, striving to honor God in all they do. Colossians 3:17 says, "And whatsoever ye do in word or deed, do all in the name of the Lord Jesus, giving thanks to God and the Father by him." This verse encourages believers to be intentional in their actions, doing everything for the glory of God.

Precision in both golf and the Christian life also involves resilience. For a golfer, achieving precision in swing mechanics requires resilience and a willingness to keep practicing and improving, even when progress seems slow. It means not giving up after a few bad shots but continuing to work on their skills and strive for better results. Similarly, Christians are called to be resilient in their faith, continuing to follow God's word and seek His guidance, even when faced with trials. Galatians 6:9 says, "And let us not be weary in well doing: for in due season we shall reap, if we faint not." This verse encourages believers to keep doing good and to persevere, trusting that their efforts will bear fruit in God's perfect timing.

Precision also involves trust. For a golfer, this means trusting in their training, their technique, and their ability to execute their swing. They rely on their preparation and practice to guide them through challenging rounds, trusting that their hard work will pay off. Similarly, Christians are called to trust in God's word and His promises, relying on His guidance and strength to live a life that honors Him. Proverbs 3:5-6 says, "Trust in the LORD with all thine heart; and lean not unto thine own understanding. In all thy ways acknowledge him, and he shall direct thy paths." This verse encourages believers to trust in God and follow His direction, knowing that He will guide them with precision and care.

In both golf and the Christian life, precision is also about integrity. For a golfer, this means playing the game with honesty and fairness, adhering to the rules and respecting the spirit of the game. Precision in swing mechanics requires golfers to be truthful about their performance and to strive for improvement with integrity. Similarly, Christians are called to live with integrity, following God's word with honesty and sincerity. Psalm 25:21 says, "Let integrity and uprightness preserve me; for I wait on thee." This verse highlights the importance of integrity in the Christian life, encouraging believers to uphold their values and live truthfully.

In conclusion, precision is a vital quality in both golf and the Christian life, involving a commitment to learning and improvement, attention to detail, discipline and consistency, patience and perseverance, humility, intentionality, trust, and integrity. For a golfer, achieving precision in swing mechanics means paying close attention to the details of their swing, practicing consistently, staying disciplined, being patient and persevering through challenges, staying humble and teachable, being intentional with their actions, trusting in their training, and playing with integrity. This precision helps golfers achieve better accuracy, consistency, and overall performance in their game. Similarly, in the Christian life, precision in spiritual actions involves studying the Bible, applying its teachings with care, practicing self-discipline, living with humility, making intentional choices, persevering in faith, trusting in God's guidance, and living with integrity. Colossians 3:17 says, "And whatsoever ye do in word or deed, do all in the name of the Lord Jesus, giving thanks to God and the Father by him." By committing to precision in their respective pursuits, both golfers and Christians can achieve their goals, grow in their skills and faith, and live lives that honor God. Precision is a journey marked by continuous effort, attention to detail, and a commitment to excellence, leading to success and fulfillment in both golf and the Christian life.

Chapter 23 Perspective

Perspective is crucial in both golf and the Christian life, as it allows individuals to remain focused, calm, and resilient amidst challenges and setbacks. For a golfer, keeping the right perspective during the game is essential for maintaining composure and enjoyment. Golf is a sport filled with ups and downs, where players often face difficult shots, unpredictable weather, and tough course conditions. A golfer with the right perspective understands that a single bad shot or even a bad hole does not define their entire game or their skill level. They recognize that golf is a game of averages, where consistency over the entire round is more important than any individual shot. By keeping a long-term perspective, golfers can avoid getting overly frustrated by mistakes and can focus on recovering and making the next shot better. This perspective helps them stay calm, reduces anxiety, and allows them to enjoy the game more fully. Similarly, in the Christian life, keeping an eternal perspective is vital for navigating the trials and tribulations of life. Christians are encouraged to focus on the bigger picture, understanding that their current struggles are temporary and that their ultimate goal is to live in accordance with God's will and to attain eternal life with Him. Colossians 3:2 says, "Set your affection on things above, not on things on the earth." This verse reminds believers to focus on spiritual and eternal matters rather than getting overly concerned with earthly problems and material possessions.

In both golf and the Christian life, perspective involves focusing on what truly matters. For a golfer, this means understanding that while winning tournaments and achieving good scores are important, the true value of the game lies in the enjoyment, the challenge, and the personal growth it offers. Golfers who maintain this perspective are able to find joy in the process, regardless of the outcome of any particular game. They appreciate the beauty of the course, the camaraderie with fellow players, and the satisfaction of improving their skills. Similarly, Christians are called to focus on their relationship with God and the spiritual growth they experience through their faith. This means prioritizing their spiritual well-being over worldly concerns and trusting that God is in control. Matthew 6:33 says, "But seek ye first the kingdom of God, and his righteousness; and all these things shall be added unto you." This verse encourages believers to focus on God's kingdom and righteousness, trusting that He will provide for their needs.

Perspective also involves maintaining a positive outlook. For a golfer, keeping a positive perspective means looking at mistakes as learning opportunities and focusing on their strengths rather than their weaknesses. A positive attitude helps golfers stay motivated, recover quickly from setbacks, and maintain confidence in their abilities. They remind themselves of their good shots and progress, which helps them stay focused and perform better. Similarly, Christians are encouraged to maintain a positive perspective by focusing on God's promises and faithfulness. Romans 8:28 says, "And we know that all things work together for good to them that love God, to them who are the called according to his purpose." This verse reassures believers that God is working for their good, even in difficult circumstances, and encourages them to trust in His plan.

In both golf and the Christian life, perspective involves gratitude. For a golfer, being grateful for the opportunity to play, the beauty of the course, and the camaraderie with fellow players helps create a positive and fulfilling experience. Gratitude helps golfers appreciate the game, regardless of their performance, and keeps them grounded in the joy of playing. Similarly, Christians are called to cultivate an attitude of gratitude, recognizing and giving thanks for God's blessings in their lives. 1 Thessalonians 5:18 says, "In every thing give thanks: for this is the will of God in Christ Jesus concerning you." This verse highlights the importance of gratitude in the Christian life, encouraging believers to give thanks in all circumstances, which fosters a sense of peace and contentment.

Perspective in both golf and the Christian life also involves keeping a balanced view of success and failure. For a golfer, this means understanding that both success and failure are part of the game and that neither should be taken too seriously. They recognize that every golfer, no matter how skilled, experiences bad shots and poor rounds. By keeping a balanced perspective, golfers can stay motivated to improve without becoming discouraged by setbacks. Similarly, Christians are called to maintain a balanced perspective on their spiritual journey, understanding that growth and progress often come through trials and challenges. James 1:2-4 says, "My brethren, count it all joy when ye fall into divers temptations; knowing this, that the trying of your faith worketh patience. But let patience have her perfect work, that ye may be perfect and entire, wanting nothing." This passage encourages believers to view challenges as opportunities for growth and to trust that God is using their experiences to develop their character and faith.

Perspective also involves trust and faith. For a golfer, this means trusting in their training, their skills, and their ability to execute their shots. They rely on their preparation and practice to guide them through challenging rounds, trusting that their hard work will pay off. This trust helps golfers stay calm and focused, even under pressure. Similarly, Christians are called to trust in God's word and His promises, relying on His guidance and strength to navigate life's challenges. Proverbs 3:5-6 says, "Trust in the LORD with all thine heart; and lean not unto thine own understanding. In all thy ways acknowledge him, and he shall direct thy paths." This verse encourages believers to trust in God and follow His direction, knowing that He will lead them on the right path.

In both golf and the Christian life, perspective also involves learning and growth. For a golfer, maintaining the right perspective means viewing each game as an opportunity to learn and improve. They analyze their performance, identify areas for improvement, and make adjustments to their technique. This mindset helps them stay motivated and committed to their development, even when progress is slow. Similarly, Christians are called to view their spiritual journey as a continuous process of learning and growth. This involves studying the Bible, applying its teachings, and seeking to deepen their relationship with God. 2 Timothy 2:15 says, "Study to shew thyself approved unto God, a workman that needeth not to be ashamed, rightly dividing the word of truth." This verse highlights the importance of diligent study and application of God's word, encouraging believers to grow in their knowledge and faith.

In both golf and the Christian life, perspective also involves resilience. For a golfer, this means bouncing back from bad shots or tough rounds, staying positive, and continuing to play their best. They understand that setbacks are part of the game and that resilience is key to overcoming challenges and achieving success. This resilience is developed through experience, practice, and a positive mindset. Similarly, Christians are called to be resilient in their faith, trusting that God is with them and will help them overcome trials. Philippians 4:13 says, "I can do all things through Christ which strengtheneth me." This verse encourages believers to rely on Christ's strength and to persevere through challenges with confidence and faith.

Perspective also involves empathy and understanding. For a golfer, this means understanding that everyone has their own struggles and challenges on the course and being supportive and encouraging to fellow players. This empathy fosters a sense of camaraderie and sportsmanship, enhancing the overall enjoyment of the game. Similarly, Christians are called to show empathy and understanding toward one another, being sensitive to each other's needs and emotions. Romans 12:15 says, "Rejoice with them that do rejoice, and weep with them that weep." This verse encourages believers to share in each other's joys and sorrows, fostering a deep sense of community and compassion.

In both golf and the Christian life, perspective also involves keeping a long-term view. For a golfer, this means understanding that improvement takes time and that each round is just one step in a longer journey of development. They focus on their long-term goals and progress, recognizing that setbacks are temporary and that persistence and hard work will lead to success. Similarly, Christians are encouraged to maintain an eternal perspective, trusting that their current struggles are temporary and that their ultimate hope is in Christ. 2 Corinthians 4:17-18 says, "For our light affliction, which is but for a moment, worketh for us a far more exceeding and eternal weight of glory; While we look not at the things which are seen, but at the things which are not seen: for the things which are seen are temporal; but the things which are not seen are eternal." This passage encourages believers to focus on the eternal rewards and to trust that their current struggles are part of God's greater plan.

In conclusion, perspective is a vital quality in both golf and the Christian life, involving a focus on what truly matters, maintaining a positive outlook, practicing gratitude, keeping a balanced view of success and failure, trusting in God's plan, continuous learning and growth, resilience, empathy, and keeping a long-term view. For a golfer, keeping the right perspective during the game means focusing on the enjoyment and personal growth the game offers, staying positive, being grateful, and viewing each game as a learning opportunity. This perspective helps golfers stay calm, motivated, and resilient, allowing them to perform better and enjoy the game more. Similarly, in the Christian life, keeping an eternal perspective involves focusing on spiritual and eternal matters, maintaining a positive outlook, practicing gratitude, trusting in God's plan, and viewing challenges as opportunities for growth. Colossians 3:2 says, "Set your affection on things above, not on things on the earth." By committing to the right perspective in their respective pursuits, both golfers and Christians can navigate challenges effectively, achieve their goals, and experience greater joy and fulfillment. Perspective is a journey marked by continuous effort, trust, gratitude, and a commitment to maintaining a balanced and positive outlook, leading to success and satisfaction in both golf and the Christian life.

Chapter 24 Prayer

Prayer is an essential practice for both golfers and Christians, offering strength, focus, and a deeper connection with God. For a golfer, praying for strength and focus can be a vital part of their preparation and mindset during a game. Golf is a mentally demanding sport that requires concentration, patience, and resilience. Praying before and during a round can help golfers stay calm and centered, allowing them to approach each shot with clarity and confidence. It provides a moment of peace and reflection, helping to block out distractions and maintain focus on the task at hand. When faced with challenging shots or difficult conditions, prayer can offer the mental fortitude needed to persevere and stay positive. For many golfers, prayer is a way to seek God's guidance and support, trusting that He is with them in every moment, helping them to perform to the best of their abilities. Similarly, in the Christian life, prayer is a fundamental practice that strengthens faith and deepens one's relationship with God. Christians are called to pray constantly, seeking God's presence, guidance, and support in all aspects of their lives. 1 Thessalonians 5:17 says, "Pray without ceasing." This verse encourages believers to maintain a continuous dialogue with God, making prayer an integral part of their daily routine.

In both golf and the Christian life, prayer involves seeking strength and guidance. For a golfer, this means asking for the mental and emotional strength to handle the pressures of the game, to stay focused, and to make wise decisions. Prayer can be a source of comfort and reassurance, reminding golfers that they are not alone and that they can rely on God's strength to carry them through challenging moments. This connection with God can help golfers maintain a positive attitude and resilience, even when faced with setbacks. Similarly, Christians turn to prayer for strength and guidance in their spiritual journey. Through prayer, they seek God's wisdom, direction, and support, trusting that He will provide for their needs and help them navigate life's challenges. Psalm 28:7 says, "The Lord is my strength and my shield; my heart trusted in him, and I am helped: therefore my heart greatly rejoiceth; and with my song will I praise him." This verse highlights the protective and supportive nature of God's presence, encouraging believers to trust in His strength.

Prayer also involves gratitude and thanksgiving. For a golfer, expressing gratitude through prayer can help maintain a positive mindset and a sense of appreciation for the opportunity to play. Thanking God for the beauty of the course, the joy of the game, and the camaraderie with fellow players fosters a spirit of gratitude that enhances the overall experience. This gratitude helps golfers stay grounded and focused on the positive aspects of the game, regardless of their performance. Similarly, Christians are encouraged to express gratitude in their prayers, recognizing and thanking God for His blessings and provisions. Philippians 4:6 says, "Be careful for nothing; but in every thing by prayer and supplication with thanksgiving let your requests be made known unto God." This verse emphasizes the importance of combining requests with thanksgiving, fostering a heart of gratitude and trust in God's goodness.

In both golf and the Christian life, prayer is a means of seeking peace and calm. For a golfer, prayer can provide a moment of tranquility before a critical shot, helping to calm nerves and reduce anxiety. By focusing on God's presence and seeking His peace, golfers can approach their game with a sense of calm and confidence. This peace helps them to remain composed under pressure, enabling them to perform better and enjoy the game more fully. Similarly, Christians turn to prayer to find peace amidst the busyness and challenges of life. Philippians 4:7 says, "And the peace of God, which passeth all understanding, shall keep your hearts and minds through Christ Jesus." This verse assures believers that God's peace will guard their hearts and minds, providing a sense of calm and assurance in every situation.

Prayer also involves intercession and support for others. For a golfer, praying for their fellow players, coaches, and caddies fosters a sense of community and mutual support. This intercessory prayer can strengthen relationships and create a positive and encouraging atmosphere on the course. Similarly, Christians are called to pray for one another, lifting up their needs and concerns before God. James 5:16 says, "Confess your faults one to another, and pray one for another, that ye may be healed. The effectual fervent prayer of a righteous man availeth much." This verse highlights the power of intercessory prayer, encouraging believers to support and uplift each other through prayer.

In both golf and the Christian life, prayer involves seeking alignment with God's will. For a golfer, this means seeking God's guidance in their decisions and actions on the course, asking for the wisdom to make the right choices and the strength to execute their plans. This alignment with God's will helps golfers approach their game with a sense of purpose and direction, trusting that God is guiding their steps. Similarly, Christians seek to align their lives with God's will through prayer, asking for His guidance and direction in all aspects of their lives. Matthew 6:10 says, "Thy kingdom come, Thy will be done in earth, as it is in heaven." This verse emphasizes the importance of seeking God's will and surrendering to His plans, trusting that His purposes are good and perfect.

Prayer in both golf and the Christian life also involves confession and seeking forgiveness. For a golfer, this might mean acknowledging their mistakes and shortcomings on the course, asking for the humility to learn and grow from them. This confession helps golfers maintain a humble and teachable attitude, fostering a spirit of continuous improvement. Similarly, Christians are called to confess their sins and seek God's forgiveness through prayer. 1 John 1:9 says, "If we confess our sins, he is faithful and just to forgive us our sins, and to cleanse us from all unrighteousness." This verse assures believers of God's forgiveness and cleansing, encouraging them to come before Him with honesty and repentance.

In both golf and the Christian life, prayer involves seeking God's presence and connection. For a golfer, taking a moment to pray on the course can foster a sense of closeness with God, reminding them of His presence and support. This connection helps golfers stay focused on what truly matters and find joy in their game. Similarly, Christians seek to deepen their relationship with God through prayer, desiring to experience His presence and fellowship. Psalm 16:11 says, "Thou wilt shew me the path of life: in thy presence is fulness of joy; at thy right hand there are pleasures for evermore." This verse highlights the joy and fulfillment found in God's presence, encouraging believers to seek Him continually.

In conclusion, prayer is a vital practice in both golf and the Christian life, involving seeking strength and guidance, expressing gratitude, finding peace, interceding for others, aligning with God's will, confessing sins, and seeking God's presence. For a golfer, praying for strength and focus can enhance their mental and emotional resilience, helping them to stay calm and perform better. Prayer provides a moment of tranquility, fostering a positive mindset and a sense of connection with God. Similarly, in the Christian life, constant prayer is essential for spiritual growth and maintaining a close relationship with God. Christians are called to pray without ceasing, seeking God's guidance, expressing gratitude, finding peace, interceding for others, aligning with His will, confessing sins, and experiencing His presence. 1 Thessalonians 5:17 says, "Pray without ceasing." By committing to a life of prayer, both golfers and Christians can navigate their respective journeys with greater strength, focus, and joy, trusting in God's presence and guidance every step of the way. Prayer is a journey marked by continuous effort, trust, gratitude, and a commitment to maintaining a deep connection with God, leading to success and fulfillment in both golf and the Christian life.

Chapter 25 Perfection

Perfection is a lofty goal that both golfers and Christians strive towards, whether it's achieving the perfect game or attaining spiritual perfection. For a golfer, striving for the perfect game involves honing every aspect of their play, from their swing mechanics and putting to their mental approach and physical conditioning. The pursuit of perfection in golf is a journey of continuous improvement, requiring dedication, discipline, and a relentless focus on refining skills and strategies. Golfers aim to minimize errors, improve consistency, and achieve a level of play where every shot is executed with precision and accuracy. This quest for perfection is not just about achieving a flawless scorecard, but also about the personal satisfaction and sense of accomplishment that comes from mastering the game. Golfers practice tirelessly, often seeking the guidance of coaches and using technology to analyze their performance. They study the nuances of the game, learn from their mistakes, and make adjustments to enhance their play. This commitment to perfection drives them to push their limits and continually seek ways to improve. Similarly, in the Christian life, striving for spiritual perfection is about growing in faith and aligning one's life with God's will. Christians are called to emulate the character of Jesus, seeking to live a life of holiness, love, and obedience to God. Matthew 5:48 says, "Be ye therefore perfect, even as your Father which is in heaven is perfect." This verse challenges believers to aim for spiritual maturity and completeness, reflecting the perfection of their Heavenly Father.

In both golf and the Christian life, the pursuit of perfection involves setting high standards and working diligently to meet them. For a golfer, this means setting goals for improvement and developing a practice regimen that targets specific areas of their game. They break down their swing mechanics, analyze their putting technique, and work on their mental game to enhance focus and resilience. By setting clear, achievable goals, golfers can track their progress and stay motivated on their journey towards perfection. Similarly, Christians set spiritual goals to grow in their faith, such as deepening their understanding of the Bible, improving their prayer life, and demonstrating Christ-like behavior in their interactions with others. These goals help believers stay focused on their spiritual growth and measure their progress towards becoming more like Jesus.

The pursuit of perfection also involves perseverance and resilience. For a golfer, achieving perfection requires overcoming setbacks, learning from mistakes, and maintaining a positive attitude despite challenges. Golf is a game of highs and lows, where even the best players experience bad shots and tough rounds. The key to striving for perfection is to stay resilient, using each setback as an opportunity to learn and improve. Golfers understand that perfection is a journey, not a destination, and they remain committed to their goals even when progress seems slow. Similarly, Christians are called to persevere in their faith, trusting that God is with them and will help them overcome obstacles. James 1:4 says, "But let patience have her perfect work, that ye may be perfect and entire, wanting nothing." This verse encourages believers to endure trials with patience, knowing that these experiences help them grow towards spiritual perfection.

In both golf and the Christian life, the pursuit of perfection involves attention to detail. For a golfer, this means focusing on the finer points of their technique, such as grip, stance, and alignment. They pay close attention to their swing plane, the tempo of their swing, and the contact with the ball, understanding that small adjustments can lead to significant improvements. This meticulous approach helps golfers refine their skills and achieve greater consistency. Similarly, Christians are called to pay attention to the details of their spiritual lives, ensuring that their thoughts, words, and actions align with God's teachings. This involves studying the Bible, reflecting on its teachings, and applying them to everyday life. Colossians 3:17 says, "And whatsoever ye do in word or deed, do all in the name of the Lord Jesus, giving thanks to God and the Father by him." This verse emphasizes the importance of doing everything with a heart of gratitude and a commitment to honoring God.

The pursuit of perfection also involves humility. For a golfer, humility means recognizing that there is always room for improvement and being open to feedback and instruction. It involves acknowledging mistakes and learning from them, rather than becoming discouraged or arrogant. Humility helps golfers stay grounded and focused on their continuous development. Similarly, Christians are called to live with humility, recognizing their need for God's grace and guidance. Philippians 2:3 says, "Let nothing be done through strife or vainglory; but in lowliness of mind let each esteem other better than themselves." This verse encourages believers to approach their spiritual journey with humility, valuing others and relying on God's wisdom.

In both golf and the Christian life, the pursuit of perfection involves patience. For a golfer, mastering the game takes time and consistent effort. They understand that improvement is a gradual process, and they remain patient as they work towards their goals. This patience helps them stay committed and motivated, even when progress seems slow. Similarly, Christians are called to be patient in their spiritual growth, trusting that God is working in their lives to help them become more like Him. Romans 8:25 says, "But if we hope for that we see not, then do we with patience wait for it." This verse encourages believers to wait patiently for God's promises, knowing that spiritual growth is a journey that requires time and perseverance.

The pursuit of perfection also involves trust. For a golfer, this means trusting in their training, their skills, and their ability to perform under pressure. They rely on their preparation and practice to guide them through challenging rounds, trusting that their hard work will pay off. This trust helps golfers stay calm and focused, even under pressure. Similarly, Christians are called to trust in God's word and

His promises, relying on His guidance and strength to navigate life's challenges. Proverbs 3:5-6 says, "Trust in the LORD with all thine heart; and lean not unto thine own understanding. In all thy ways acknowledge him, and he shall direct thy paths." This verse encourages believers to trust in God and follow His direction, knowing that He will lead them on the right path.

In both golf and the Christian life, the pursuit of perfection also involves integrity. For a golfer, this means playing the game with honesty and fairness, adhering to the rules and respecting the spirit of the game. Precision in swing mechanics requires golfers to be truthful about their performance and to strive for improvement with integrity. Similarly, Christians are called to live with integrity, following God's word with honesty and sincerity. Psalm 25:21 says, "Let integrity and uprightness preserve me; for I wait on thee." This verse highlights the importance of integrity in the Christian life, encouraging believers to uphold their values and live truthfully.

In conclusion, the pursuit of perfection is a vital quality in both golf and the Christian life, involving a commitment to learning and improvement, attention to detail, discipline and consistency, patience and perseverance, humility, trust, and integrity. For a golfer, striving for the perfect game means paying close attention to the details of their swing, practicing consistently, staying disciplined, being patient and persevering through challenges, staying humble and teachable, being intentional with their actions, trusting in their training, and playing with integrity. This precision helps golfers achieve better accuracy, consistency, and overall performance in their game. Similarly, in the Christian life, striving for spiritual perfection involves studying the Bible, applying its teachings with care, practicing self-discipline, living with humility, making intentional choices, persevering in faith, trusting in God's guidance, and living with integrity. Matthew 5:48 says, "Be ye therefore perfect, even as your Father which is in heaven is perfect." By committing to perfection in their respective pursuits, both golfers and

Christians can achieve their goals, grow in their skills and faith, and live lives that honor God. The pursuit of perfection is a journey marked by continuous effort, attention to detail, and a commitment to excellence, leading to success and fulfillment in both golf and the Christian life.

Don't miss out!

Visit the website below and you can sign up to receive emails whenever Joshua Rhoades publishes a new book. There's no charge and no obligation.

https://books2read.com/r/B-A-AJLBB-OTHWE

Connecting independent readers to independent writers.

Did you love *Par for the Course- Faith and Fairways*? Then you should read *From Dugout to Devotion- Spiritual Lessons from Baseball*[1] by Joshua Rhoades!

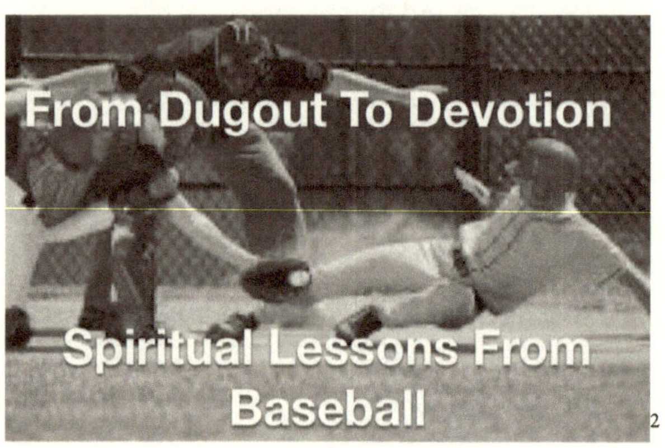

[2]

"From Dugout to Devotion: Spiritual Lessons from Baseball" invites you to step onto the diamond not just as a fan of the game, but as a seeker of deeper truths. Baseball is more than just a sport; it's a reflection of life itself, filled with moments of triumph, defeat, perseverance, and grace. As the bat cracks against the ball and the crowd holds its breath, there's more at play than just the game. Beneath the surface, baseball is rich with spiritual parallels that speak to the heart of our faith journey.

In every pitch, swing, and catch, there are lessons that echo the very principles of our Christian walk. The dugout, a place of preparation and strategy, mirrors our need for spiritual readiness and the importance of being grounded in God's Word. Just as players study their opponents and prepare for the game, we too must equip ourselves with spiritual wisdom and understanding to navigate the challenges we face in life. The devotion that drives a player to train, to push through

---

1. https://books2read.com/u/mdEJ0X

2. https://books2read.com/u/mdEJ0X

pain and fatigue, mirrors the perseverance we are called to have in our faith—a devotion to God that requires discipline, dedication, and trust.

This book takes you on a journey through the innings of life, drawing out spiritual insights from the game of baseball that can transform your walk with the Lord. It's about more than just the love of the game; it's about finding God's hand in every play, every challenge, and every victory. Whether you're standing in the batter's box, facing a curveball life has thrown your way, or running the bases, striving toward your goals, the lessons gleaned from baseball can guide you in your spiritual journey.

Through the pages of "From Dugout to Devotion," you'll discover how the discipline, teamwork, and perseverance required on the field are the same virtues needed in our spiritual lives. The patience of waiting for the right pitch, the courage to swing even when the outcome is uncertain, and the resilience to get back up after a strikeout all mirror the spiritual truths we encounter in our walk with Christ. Each chapter delves into these parallels, offering encouragement, wisdom, and practical applications to help you grow in your faith.

Whether you're a lifelong baseball fan or new to the sport, this book will open your eyes to the deeper spiritual lessons that can be found in the game. It will challenge you to see your faith in a new light, to draw strength from the timeless truths embedded in the game, and to apply these lessons to your own life. As you turn the pages, you'll be inspired to approach your faith with the same passion and dedication that drives a baseball player to strive for excellence. "From Dugout to Devotion" is more than just a book—it's a call to deepen your relationship with God through the timeless lessons found in America's favorite pastime. So, step up to the plate, and let the game begin.

www.ingramcontent.com/pod-product-compliance
Lightning Source LLC
Chambersburg PA
CBHW022139150726
47992CB00002B/668